CAST

(*In order of speaking*)

PTOLEMY
PERDICCAS
MAZARES
ALEXANDER
PYTHIA OF DELPHI
HEPHAESTION
PHILOTAS
AN ATTENDANT
DARIUS, KING OF PERSIA
BESSUS
QUEEN-MOTHER OF PERSIA
QUEEN STATIRA OF PERSIA
PRINCESS STATIRA OF PERSIA
CLEITUS
PARMENION
PALACE OFFICIAL
ROXANA
GREEK SOLDIERS
PERSIAN SOLDIERS

Adventure Story was first produced at the St. James's Theatre, London, on March 17th, 1949, with the following cast:

PTOLEMY	*Raymond Westwell*
PERDICCAS	*Antony Baird*
MAZARES	*Marne Maitland*
ALEXANDER	*Paul Scofield*
PYTHIA OF DELPHI	*Veronica Turleigh*
HEPHAESTION	*Julian Dallas*
PHILOTAS	*Robert Flemyng*
AN ATTENDANT	*Natasha Wills*
DARIUS, KING OF PERSIA	*Noel Willman*
BESSUS	*William Devlin*
QUEEN MOTHER OF PERSIA	*Gwen Ffrangcon-Davies*
QUEEN STATIRA OF PERSIA	*Hazel Terry*
PRINCESS STATIRA OF PERSIA	*June Rodney*
CLEITUS	*Cecil Trouncer*
PARMENION	*Nicholas Hannen*
PALACE OFFICIAL	*Walter Gotell*
ROXANA	*Joy Parker*
GREEK SOLDIERS	*Stanley Baker* *John Van Eyssen* *Terence Longdon*
PERSIAN SOLDIERS	*David Oxley* *Frederick Treves*

The play produced by PETER GLENVILLE

Decor by GEORGES WAKHEVITCH

Music specially composed by BENJAMIN FRANKEL

SYNOPSIS OF SCENES

The action of the play extends from 336 B.C. to 323 B.C.

PROLOGUE: Babylon

ACT I

SCENE 1 ... Delphi
SCENE 2 ... Babylon
SCENE 3 ... Issus (the tent)
SCENE 4 ... Babylon
SCENE 5 ... Gaugemela (the tent)

ACT II

SCENE 1 ... Parthia
SCENE 2 ... Bactria (the tent)
SCENE 3 ... Babylon
SCENE 4 ... Alexandria-at-the-end-of-the-world (the tent)
SCENE 5 ... The same

EPILOGUE: Babylon

FOR
WILLIAM CHAPPELL

ADVENTURE STORY

PROLOGUE

A courtyard at night. In the centre is a litter supported by two soldiers on which lies the dying ALEXANDER. *Round the litter stand five people, patiently watching, their faces barely discernible. They are* ROXANA, *the* QUEEN-MOTHER OF PERSIA, PERDICCAS, PTOLEMY *and* MAZARES. *The last is holding the wrist of the man in the bed, and is bending his ear over his heart. When he straightens himself, he nods to Perdiccas. The older of the two women gasps and is comforted by the younger who takes her in her arms.* PERDICCAS *exchanges a glance with* PTOLEMY *and then steps forward slowly to the side of the bed. He kneels down.*

PERDICCAS. Sir? [*Louder*] Sir? [*There is no answer.*] This is Perdiccas. Can you hear me? [*He bends his head close to the other's.*] This is Perdiccas, sir. Make a sign if you understand. [*The hands cease their movement for a second and one of them is weakly raised an inch or two from the coverlet. Then it falls limply back.*] Will you name your successor?

PTOLEMY *comes up to him.*

PTOLEMY [*eagerly*]. Well?

PERDICCAS *shakes his head.*

PTOLEMY. Try again.

PERDICCAS [*louder*]. Sir—the time has come for you to name your successor. Who is it to be?

Both PERDICCAS *and* PTOLEMY *kneel now, to catch the reply. There is none. The hands continue to twist and turn.*

PTOLEMY. This is Ptolemy. Am I to succeed you? Make a sign. [*There is no sign.*] Perdiccas, then?—Craterus? Your child to be? [*To Perdiccas.*] He said something.

PERDICCAS. His lips moved——

PTOLEMY [*to* ALEXANDER]. We didn't hear that. Will you repeat it?

PERDICCAS. Repeat what you said, sir. Who is to be your successor?

Again they listen. MAZARES *approaches and feels his patient's wrist.*

PTOLEMY. Speak again, sir. Who is to succeed you? Who?

MAZARES. Later, please. No more now.

PTOLEMY *and* PERDICCAS *get to their feet.*

PTOLEMY [*to* PERDICCAS]. Did you hear anything?

PERDICCAS. No.

PTOLEMY. He certainly said something. It sounded almost like "Who shall I condemn to death?"

PERDICCAS. Something like that.

PTOLEMY [*to* MAZARES]. What are the chances of his regaining his senses before—— [MAZARES *shrugs his shoulders.*] [*To* PERDICCAS] We must try again. We must.

PERDICCAS [*in a dead voice*]. Yes. I suppose it's important.

PTOLEMY [*shortly*]. Important! [*There is a distant sound of men's voices, then a barked order.*] Can't you stop them making that din?

PERDICCAS. They've been very patient. They've been out in the courtyard for ten hours——

PTOLEMY. How many are there?

PERDICCAS. Two from each company. All under-officers.

PTOLEMY. I don't like it. We don't want trouble.

PERDICCAS. There won't be trouble if they see him.

PTOLEMY. You think we should let them in now?

PERDICCAS. I do.

PTOLEMY. They could muster in the ante-room and come in one at a time, file past the bed and out. Who's in charge?

PERDICCAS. Craterus.

PTOLEMY. I'll tell him.

PTOLEMY *goes.*

QUEEN-MOTHER *moves to bed.* PERDICCAS *moves forward and looks at her.* MAZARES *now joins them and the four of them, grouped round the bed, gaze down at the dying man.* QUEEN-MOTHER *turns to* ROXANA, *who comforts her.*

There is a pause, and then suddenly ALEXANDER'S *voice—a gentle whisper—fills the theatre with sound. The four at the bedside do not move. It is not to them that* ALEXANDER *is speaking.*

ALEXANDER'S VOICE. So I am dying. Alexander is dying. God, oh God. Not in bed—in battle—not in bed——. Why did you never let me see that it would end in this? [PTOLEMY *enters and stands near* PERDICCAS.] Could I ever have turned back, I wonder. [PTOLEMY *beckons someone forward. A soldier steps into the light peering timidly at the occupant of the bed. The soldier salutes with his spear. Automatically a hand is weakly raised in reply. The soldier passes the bed into the darkness. Another soldier appears at the foot of the bed.*] Where did it first go wrong? [*The soldier salutes and receives the same weak reply. The soldier covers his face with his hands. Third soldier enters, kneels.*] Goodbye, my friend. Thank you for caring. [*The soldier moves out into the darkness.*] Where did it first go wrong?

THE LIGHTS FADE

ACT I

SCENE ONE

A temple in Delphi. The head of an immense statue of Apollo can be seen at the back, rising above a parapet erected high above the floor of the main part of the building which it conceals. The temple is built into the face of a mountain and the chamber we are now looking at has two doors R. and L., one of which (R.) seems to lead into a cavern in the rocks; the other to stairs which connect with the unseen floor of the temple.

As the lights come on the stage is empty, and there is the sound of distant music and chanting. After a moment the door at left is opened to admit the PYTHIA, *a lady of early middle age, imposingly gowned. She is followed at a distance by an attendant, who assists her to remove her ceremonial robe.* PYTHIA *turns and bows. The* ATTENDANT *bows and goes, leaving the* PYTHIA *alone. The chanting and music continue. The* PYTHIA *kneels to the statue, raising her hands in supplication. The door at left is opened and* HEPHAESTION *comes in. He is a young Macedonian officer of twenty-one. He stands at the door looking round, unaware of* PYTHIA *and suddenly sees her.*

HEPHAESTION. Madam?

The PYTHIA *looks up, but does not immediately rise.*

PYTHIA [*rising*]. You have no right in this place, sir. This is forbidden ground. I must ask you to leave at once.

HEPHAESTION. I am here under orders.

PYTHIA. No one gives orders in Delphi save the god Apollo through his chosen mouthpiece, myself.

HEPHAESTION. The matter is urgent, madam. My master has come to Delphi to consult the oracle, and must leave tonight. He demands an audience with you at once.

PYTHIA. Indeed. Then you must tell him that his demand is

refused. The mystery of the oracle is a holy boon to be craved of god, not demanded as a favour from a hired fortune-teller.

HEPHAESTION. My choice of words was unhappy. Forgive me, madam. My master piously begs the god Apollo to answer his question——

PYTHIA. Then let him ask it in the prescribed form—in a petition written to the High Council of Delphic Priests. Should his question be chosen it will, after he has undergone the necessary period of fasting and prayer, be answered to him on a day and an hour duly appointed by the god. That is all I have to tell you, sir. You may go.

She turns away.

HEPHAESTION. But madam——

PHILOTAS *comes in quickly. He is a trifle older than* HEPHAESTION, *and is obviously far less impressed by his surroundings than the other.*

PHILOTAS. What's the delay?

HEPHAESTION. I told you to stay outside.

PHILOTAS. Yes, I know. [*Looking round.*] So this is the holiest spot in Greece, is it? Rather impressive, I must admit. It reminds me of all my unrepented sins——

PYTHIA [*approaching* PHILOTAS]. Are you this man's master?

PHILOTAS [*looking at* HEPHAESTION]. In some things. Not in all. I must admit. He beats me at wrestling. But if you mean am I King Alexander I am not. My name is Philotas and he—if he hasn't told you already—is Hephaestion. We are both of us, as you have no doubt already recognised from our armour, officers of His Majesty's personal bodyguard—The Companion Cavalry.

PYTHIA. You armour, sir, is unknown to me, but your manners are unmistakably Macedonian. This King you speak of—this Alexander—is, therefore, the new King of Macedon.

PHILOTAS. He is. And Captain-General of all Greece.

PYTHIA. An imposing title for so young a man. Wasn't it his father's? I didn't realise it had become hereditary.

PHILOTAS. That insinuation is, I feel, a little unworthy of a woman of god. King Alexander was freely elected Captain-General in the late King Philip's place at Corinth a week ago.

PYTHIA. Indeed? Freely, I think you said?

PHILOTAS. Well, the elections were free. I admit that the presents we gave to the electors unhappily were not.

PYTHIA. Nor, I imagine, was the army you took to Corinth to safeguard the electors' persons from outside threats?

PHILOTAS. Madam—as you've just remarked—I'm a Macedonian. I am allowed to make jokes of that kind. But I doubt if that licence can be extended to a foreigner—even if she is the Pythia of Delphi.

PYTHIA. And how would you go about withdrawing that licence, sir? I am interested to know.

PHILOTAS [*fingering his sword*]. There are ways, madam. [PYTHIA *rings a bell.*] There are ways. King Alexander is waiting in the lobby of the temple, and desires you to come down to him at once.

ATTENDANT *enters.*

PYTHIA. I have already given my answer to King Alexander's request, sir. This officer [*indicating* HEPHAESTION] is bearing it to His Majesty himself.

HEPHAESTION. I think we'd better go, Philotas.

PHILOTAS. May I escort you down, madam?

PYTHIA. No sir. But I thank you for the offer. [*To* ATTENDANT.] Have the outer doors opened. These gentlemen are leaving.

PHILOTAS. You know—I'm surprised that so obviously sensible a lady should be prepared to run so drastic a risk.

PYTHIA [*gently*]. The only risk I run, sir, is of condoning a blasphemy—and the longer you two gentlemen remain in this holy place the greater is my peril.

PHILOTAS *makes as if to draw his sword. The* PYTHIA *confronts him placidly.* HEPHAESTION *walks forward quickly and takes* PHILOTAS' *arm.* PHILOTAS *slams his sword back into its sheath.*

PHILOTAS. A pity they don't have priests in Delphi.

He strides out, angry and defeated.

HEPHAESTION. I must apologise for my friend.

PYTHIA. He's very young.

HEPHAESTION. Oh no. He's quite old. He's twenty-seven.

PYTHIA. How old are you?

HEPHAESTION. Twenty-one. A year older than the King.

PYTHIA. You may tell your King that I mean him no discourtesy. I shall be pleased to pay my respects to him at a more appropriate time, and in a more appropriate place.

HEPHAESTION. I will. He won't be pleased, I'm afraid. You know, this is the first time I've ever failed him.

PYTHIA. Are you afraid of him?

HEPHAESTION. Afraid of Alexander? Good heavens, no. He's my best friend.

PYTHIA. I see. Aren't you very proud to have a king for a best friend?

HEPHAESTION [*lightly*]. No. I'm very proud to have Alexander for a best friend.

We hear him clatter down the stairs. PYTHIA *smiles, then turns to the* ATTENDANT.

PYTHIA. Bolt and bar the outer doors.

She nods to her in dismissal. She goes. The PYTHIA, *left alone, goes to a table, gathers up some papers and begins to study them. Then she settles down to write.*

A cloak is suddenly thrown over the parapet at the back and a moment afterwards ALEXANDER'S *head appears. He hoists himself over the parapet and jumps lightly into the inner chamber.*

The PYTHIA, *having heard nothing, remains absorbed in her work.* ALEXANDER *regards the back of her head for a moment, and then walks forward.*

ALEXANDER. Are you the Pythia? [*The* PYTHIA *turns with a gasp and rises and then reaches for a handbell on her table.*] No, please don't ring that. There's no need. Are you the Pythia?

PYTHIA. Yes. I am.

ALEXANDER. I am Alexander of Macedon.

PYTHIA. I had guessed that.

ALEXANDER. I look like my coins, do I?

PYTHIA. I have never seen one of your coins.

ALEXANDER. There aren't very many to see yet, I admit.

PYTHIA. I ordered the doors to be barred. How did you get in here?

ALEXANDER. Apollo helped me. [*He looks at statue.*]

PYTHIA. Apollo?

ALEXANDER. Yes. I always was rather good at climbing.

PYTHIA. King Alexander, you have desecrated this Temple. I must ask you to leave this place at once.

ALEXANDER. Yes. All right. I'll go in a moment, when I've got what I came for. I have been told to submit my question in writing—so I've scribbled it out for you. There. [*He hands her a document.*]

PYTHIA [*reading it*]. Is this seriously the question you wish me to put to the god Apollo?

ALEXANDER. Yes. Why? Have I spelt it wrong? Doesn't it make sense?

PYTHIA. You've spelt it quite correctly. Whether it makes sense or not is not for me to say. [*She folds the document.*] Very well, I shall put this before the Council——

ALEXANDER. But why can't you answer it now?

PYTHIA. For one reason and one reason only. Because it's impossible.

ALEXANDER. I see. I once asked my tutor how a man could become a god, and he answered: "By doing what is impossible for a man to do." Don't you want to become a goddess?

PYTHIA. No. But do you want to become a god?

ALEXANDER. If I do the impossible it won't be because I've become a god, but because I was born Alexander. If you're not going to answer my question, I'd better have it back, please. [*The* PYTHIA *gives it back to him.*] I don't want it falling into the wrong hands. [*He puts it into his tunic.*]

PYTHIA [*smiling.*] You think I keep Persian agents in the Temple?

ALEXANDER. You never know. Darius' spies are everywhere.

PYTHIA. Poor Darius! How he would tremble if he could see that. [*She points to the document.*]

ALEXANDER. Now you're making fun of me. But you'll see, Pythia, you'll see.

PYTHIA. How many men will you have?

ALEXANDER. With luck—about thirty-five thousand.

PYTHIA. And Darius?

ALEXANDER. Roughly a quarter of a million. It could be two million. He has the manpower for it. But I shall never give him the time to raise so many.

PYTHIA [*gently*]. Or perhaps the necessity.

ALEXANDER. Oh yes, you laugh at me, I know. Everyone does. But perhaps you won't laugh so much when the Persian empire crumbles into dust.

PYTHIA. The strongest empire in the world? In fact, the world, itself——

ALEXANDER. Giants can be surprised. And they can't move as fast as pygmies. Look, I'll tell you my plan. It's very simple. [*He kneels.*] I'm sending Parmenion—he was my father's Chief of Staff and mine—to secure a bridgehead across the Hellespont. Then I push with the main force straight into the interior. We should have sufficient concentration of force to match any army the local satraps can bring against us. I intend anyway to lure them into a pitched battle. When I've destroyed that force, I shall march down the coast, liberating all the Greek colonies as I go. I've got somehow to build up a sufficient force to meet the army Darius will bring against me in Syria.

PYTHIA. How do you know it'll be in Syria?

ALEXANDER. Because that's where I'll be by the time Darius can reach me. I shall have to force the Cilician Gates, of course.

PYTHIA. What are they?

ALEXANDER. The most easily defended pass in the world. A long, narrow defile where only three men can walk abreast. But I'll get through it somehow. Speed is the main thing. Asiatics don't understand speed. They expect all their opponents to fight by the book of rules. They don't know me. Not yet, anyway.

PYTHIA. No. What then?

ALEXANDER. Well then I shall meet Darius in the field, beat him and kill him, or take him prisoner——

PYTHIA. I see. Thirty-five thousand against a quarter of a million?

ALEXANDER. Yes. Mind you, I'm not saying it's going to be an easy battle to win——

PYTHIA. No. I can see that. After you've killed Darius, what will you do?

ALEXANDER. I shall found a new order in Asia.

PYTHIA. Indeed? With yourself at the head?

ALEXANDER. Yes, I suppose so. I hadn't thought. It's not important. If there's a worthier man than myself to rule this new state, let him do so. Only he must be a Greek, of course——

PYTHIA. Of course.

ALEXANDER. It will be an Hellenic world, you see. The city states, with their own customs and laws and constitutions can remain intact. Only national sovereignties will have to be given up—but that's a small price to pay for a world state and universal peace.

PYTHIA. Yes, I agree. A small price. What about the Persians and the Egyptians and the others who are not Greeks?

ALEXANDER. Oh, they'll be our partners. They'll have the same rights as the Greeks, but will have to submit to being ruled by a Greek instead of a Persian. Still, that's a small——

PYTHIA. ——price to pay for a world state and universal peace. I agree.

ALEXANDER. You think I'm mad, of course.

PYTHIA. No. Just very young.

ALEXANDER. All idealists are a little mad. Aristotle is madder than anyone.

PYTHIA. He's your tutor, isn't he?

ALEXANDER. He was. He's gone back to Athens now. He believes in the world state, too, you know.

PYTHIA. I see. And you're going to put his ideas into practice?

ALEXANDER. Yes. He doesn't approve of that.

PYTHIA. I'm not surprised.

ALEXANDER. In fact, he doesn't approve of me at all. He found me once reading a copy of the *Iliad*, and when he congratulated me on my taste in literature and asked me what I liked best about it, I told him I thought it an invaluable military manual. He was furious. No sense of humour, at all. I love Homer, as a matter of fact. Are you sure you can't answer my question?

PYTHIA. *I* can answer it, Alexander, if you like. But not the god Apollo——

ALEXANDER. If you answered it alone, it would be no. I don't blame you. Everyone in the world would agree with you——

PYTHIA. Why must you do this madness, Alexander?

ALEXANDER. I must make good my boast.

PYTHIA. What boast?

ALEXANDER. At the wedding banquet when my father married again after divorcing my mother. He made me attend, of course. He wouldn't miss a chance like that. His new father-in-law made a speech in which he said that now all King Philip's loyal subjects could at last hope for an heir to the throne. There were three hundred people there. I was alone. None of my friends had been allowed to come. I stood up and said: "Indeed? And what does that make me? A bastard?" Then I threw my wine in his face. There was rather a stir at that.

PYTHIA. I should imagine there would be.

ALEXANDER. Then my father got to his feet. He was drunk, of course. He drew his sword—quite slowly—no one stopping him—everyone silent, watching him, and then he started to come at me. I didn't draw my sword. I just stood there, waiting. Then it happened. His foot slipped in the spilt wine, and he crashed between two couches, completely disappearing from view, except for one leg stuck up in the air—his stiff leg, the wounded one. It was very funny, but no one laughed except me. I pointed to him and said: "Look, ladies and gentlemen. There is the man who is about to pass from Europe into Asia, and he can't even pass from one end of a table to another without falling. Perhaps Greece will have cause one day to rejoice when the Captaincy-General passes to his legitimate heir." I emphasized legitimate. Then I walked past all the goggling courtiers, smiling to them, and went out.

PYTHIA. That was very brave of you.

ALEXANDER. Brave? I didn't think of it as brave. I thought of it as rather witty. But I made the boast to my father, and I must fulfil it.

PYTHIA. But your father is dead.

ALEXANDER. I must fulfil it all the same. Goodbye, Pythia. Are you quite, quite determined not to answer my question?

PYTHIA. I have given you my answer.

ALEXANDER. But the god's answer? Can't you give me that? Oh,

Pythia, please! [*She shakes her head, smiling.*] Oh, I wish I had money to build the god a new temple, but the truth is my army has swallowed up my royal revenue.

PYTHIA. All of it? But have you nothing left?

ALEXANDER. Only my hopes.

PYTHIA. I shall remember that.

ALEXANDER. Pythia, please give me your answer.

PYTHIA [*laughing*]. No, no no!

ALEXANDER [*clutching her hands*]. You must. You must! If you do I shall remember you in my prayers for ever—I promise—I shall lead the virtuous life—I shall sacrifice to Apollo every night——

PYTHIA [*laughing*]. Oh, Alexander! You're invincible. [ALEXANDER, *releasing her hands, has stiffened into rigid silence.*] I shall pray to the god to let me give you his answer.

ALEXANDER [*quietly*]. Thank you. But there's no need now.

PYTHIA [*puzzled*]. But——

ALEXANDER. The oracle has already spoken.

Pause.

PYTHIA [*in a whisper*]. Invincible——

ALEXANDER. Goodbye, Pythia.

PYTHIA. That wasn't the god——

ALEXANDER. The god spoke. [*He turns to the parapet.*]

PYTHIA. Alexander, come back. I don't know if it was the god who spoke——

ALEXANDER. Well, that we shall both of us find out, one day, won't we, Pythia? [*He puts a leg over the parapet.*]

PYTHIA. My son—I only know this. Before any others, there is one conquest you must make first.

ALEXANDER. What's that, Pythia?

PYTHIA. Yourself.

ALEXANDER. Never fear. I haven't waited all the afternoon in your temple, staring at that inscription, for nothing.

PYTHIA. Know yourself, Alexander.

ALEXANDER. I know myself, Pythia.

PYTHIA. Do you, Alexander? Are you sure?

ALEXANDER. Quite, quite sure. Goodbye, Pythia, and thank you——

He disappears from sight.

PYTHIA [*calling*]. Remember, Alexander—there's always the last battle.

ALEXANDER [*off*]. I shall win it. I am invincible. Goodbye, Pythia, goodbye!

THE LIGHTS FADE

SCENE TWO

Babylon. A corner of the hanging gardens. A massive—but richly cushioned—stone chair, carved with the Persian Imperial arms, is Darius' favourite resting place during the heat of the day. He sits there now, impassively reading a document. He is a handsome man, in the early thirties. On a bench, a little apart, sit his mother and wife, whose names are respectively SISYGAMBIS *and* STATIRA. *The Queen-Mother is a woman who must once have had great beauty. She is now about fifty-five. The Queen is a timid creature half her age. They are embroidering a piece of tapestry together. A girl of ten or eleven is by the parapet at the back, looking out over the yard below.* PRINCE BESSUS, *satrap of Bactria, a burly figure of about fifty, is sitting on a divan to the left of the two ladies, nodding his head in gentle afternoon sleep.*

The QUEEN-MOTHER, *noticing* BESSUS' *somnolence, nudges* STATIRA. *The two look at him and smile, then continue their work.*

DARIUS [*at length, smiling*]. You know, this boy has the most wonderful insolence. I begin to admire him.

STATIRA. What has he done now?

DARIUS. It's a story in this despatch from Phrygia. Well authenticated, I gather——

QUEEN-MOTHER. No, Darius. Don't tell us. Find something more pleasant to talk about than the antics of a lunatic schoolboy.

DARIUS. But this is amusing. I must read it to Bessus. He'll enjoy it. [*Calling.*] Bessus—wake up.

BESSUS *opens his eyes.*

BESSUS. Your Majesty is mistaken. I was *not* asleep. I was thinking.

DARIUS. What of?

BESSUS. The coming campaign.

DARIUS. Nonsense. You were dreaming of the girls you are going to meet in Syria——

QUEEN-MOTHER [*sharply*]. Darius! [*She indicates the Princess.*]

DARIUS. There you see. You've shocked my mother, Bessus. Confess now. You were dreaming, weren't you?

BESSUS. Yes, but not of that. [*To* QUEEN-MOTHER.] It's this heat, ma'am, I'm afraid I can't get used to it. I can't imagine what Babylon must be like later on in the year.

QUEEN-MOTHER. A furnace, I believe. We always go north.

STATIRA. I suppose in your part of the empire, Prince Bessus, you shiver over fires at this time of year.

BESSUS. We do, ma'am. Even the rivers are still frozen.

DARIUS [*to* BESSUS]. This despatch comes from a spy in Gordium, where Alexander's in winter quarters. This is the interesting part. If it's true, it's rather charming. [*Reading.*] "There is a local superstition concerning the ancient farm-waggon, preserved in the Gordium citadel. According to this legend the empire of the world will go to anyone who can untie the knot which binds the ox-yoke to the pole. Alexander, in order not to disappoint the populace, decided to attempt the puzzle. In order to prevent trickery of any kind, I arranged that he should be followed by a large crowd of townspeople."

BESSUS. Clever.

DARIUS. A little too clever, I'm afraid. Listen. [*Reading.*] "After inspecting the knot for a few seconds Alexander treacherously severed it with his sword." Well, Bessus? Isn't there an element of old-world bravado about that gesture that rather pleases you?

BESSUS. I can't say that it altogether pleases me, sir. Those sort of madmen are the most dangerous.

DARIUS. Dangerous? Yes, at the head of an army a megalomaniac is always dangerous. Hardly at the head of a skirmishing force.

BESSUS. What has he had in the way of reinforcements since the battle of the Granicus?

DARIUS. A polite way of reminding me that his skirmishing force has already defeated a Persian army. [BESSUS *makes a deprecatory gesture.*] Alexander didn't win that battle, you know. That fool Arsites lost it. All reports agree that Alexander's generalship was idiotic. Hurling himself and the Companions straight at the heavy chariots—yelling Homeric battle cries. Cavalry against chariots! Imagine. I shudder to think what his losses must have been. Incidentally—answering your question—his reinforcements since have been negligible.

PRINCESS [*turning from the parapet*]. Father, I counted sixty-two more tents today.

DARIUS. Did you, my child? That's very clever of you. [*To* BESSUS.] That'll be the Parthian cavalry contingent. They were due this morning.

BESSUS. What cavalry strength does that give you?

DARIUS. Just short of fifty thousand.

BESSUS. Out of a total strength of three hundred thousand. That's a fair proportion.

DARIUS. It should be enough.

QUEEN-MOTHER. I don't understand why you're making this gigantic effort, Darius——

DARIUS. We don't want another Granicus——

QUEEN-MOTHER. That clever General Charidemus had the best idea. Just leave the boy to rot in Phrygia. He can't get through the Cilician Gates. After a bit he'd have got tired and gone home and you'd have saved yourself a lot of money.

DARIUS. I'm afraid my prestige would hardly allow me to do that, my dear. I can assure you I have no wish to go campaigning, but that defeat has got to be avenged. What shall I do with Alexander when I've caught him, my child?

PRINCESS [*after due thought*]. Put him in a cage with Marduk.

BESSUS. Who's Marduk?

DARIUS. Her pet lion cub. [*To* PRINCESS.] Are you taking Marduk with you?

STATIRA. No, Darius. I've told her she can't.

DARIUS. I don't see why not——

QUEEN-MOTHER. I'm certainly not having him in my quarters.

BESSUS. I didn't realize you were taking your family, sir.

DARIUS. Didn't you, Bessus? You should know I wouldn't be parted from them—even for three months——

BESSUS. Is your Majesty quite sure of the wisdom—after all, accidents can happen——

STATIRA. What accidents?

BESSUS. Epidemics—bad roads.

QUEEN-MOTHER. Nonsense, Bessus. We women like to see the world from a different vantage point than the palace in Babylon. I rather enjoy these outings.

DARIUS [*meaningly*]. Are *you* going on this campaign entirely unaccompanied, Bessus?

BESSUS [*confused*]. Well—sir—not only is the young lady quite accustomed to hardship, but she's also very useful at—er—secretarial work and that sort of thing—I mean——

DARIUS. I think, perhaps, we'd better leave the subject—don't you? [*To* QUEEN-MOTHER.] What would you like to do with the captive Alexander, mother?

QUEEN-MOTHER. Kill him, of course.

DARIUS. No. I think I shall make a friend of him. He would rather amuse me——

QUEEN-MOTHER [*shocked*]. Darius! A barbarian?

BESSUS. I believe they talk of *us* as barbarians.

DARIUS. Yes, they do, and for an interesting reason. Politically they're a very backward race. They've never advanced beyond the idea of the democratic city-state which we left behind centuries ago. [*A palace official* (MAZARES) *has entered and* now *kneels before* DARIUS, *placing his forehead on the ground. Then he hands him a document.* DARIUS *takes it without glancing at him.* MAZARES *backs out.*] The result of course is that they kill each other off by the thousands every year, in what we would call civil wars and they call national wars. A world empire like ours in which there has been no serious fighting for over two hundred years is so far beyond their ken that they have to dub us barbarians to save their political self-respect. And yet their literature is not disreputable and their art and architecture—though rather too formal for my taste—has a certain primitive strength that—— [*He has been reading the despatch and now stops short. There is a long pause. Then he looks up.*]

QUEEN-MOTHER. What is it, Darius?

DARIUS. He's broken through the Cilician Gates. [*Pause.*]

BESSUS. How did he do it?

DARIUS. Surprise attack. He covered seventy miles in two days. Impossible, isn't it?

BESSUS. Impossible. [*Pause.*]

DARIUS [*slowly*]. You know, I'm looking forward to meeting this young man. I'm looking forward to it very much indeed——

THE LIGHTS FADE

SCENE THREE

The tent of Darius. It is large and regally sumptuous. The Great Kings of Persia, even while on active service, lived in a style and agrandeur which has hardly been seen in the world since, and the furnishings and objects that we now see are of an opulence and luxury that give the tent more the appearance of a throne room in a palace than of a commander-in-chief's headquarters in the field.

There is, in fact, a throne R., carved and canopied, where Darius, no doubt, was wont to hold his levees and dispense his military justice. A low table in the centre is loaded with gold beakers, gold goblets and gold plate. Three divans surround it.

There is an aperture L. that leads into Darius' sleeping quarters and the main entrance to the tent is at the back. Here two Greek soldiers stand. Through this, at the moment, we can see the evening sky, which seems tinged with a fitful red glow, and we can hear the continued and distant sound of men's voices, raised excitedly, occasionally cheering, plainly exultant.

Oblivious of the clamour and evidently enjoying his unwonted surroundings, a ferociously-bearded and grizzled Greek veteran reclines on one of the divans, gorging himself with the food displayed thereon, and gulping great draughts of wine. This is CLEITUS, *a high officer of the Macedonian Infantry. He still bears on him the stains of battle, including a gash on his leg. He is being waited on by an imperturbable Persian servant,* MAZARES, *whom we have seen in the previous scene and therefore know to belong to Darius' personal staff.*

A woman's scream distantly rings out through the confused din of men's voices, followed by a roar of laughter. CLEITUS *nods, smiling grimly to himself. He thrusts his cup out and the* SERVANT *instantly refills it. He thrusts his hand out and grabs some more food. A gold box of sweetmeats takes his attention. He empties the sweets on to the table, thrusts the box into his tunic and con-*

tinues eating. The dish from which he is taking food also appears to prick his fancy suddenly, for he empties it quickly on to the table, wipes it on his cloak, and puts that too into his tunic. The SERVANT *politely hands him another dish.* CLEITUS *throws it savagely away to the corner of the tent.*

CLEITUS [*growling*]. Are you trying to be funny? That mightn't be so healthy, you know——

SERVANT. No, master, I do not try to be funny. I only try to serve you.

CLEITUS. Oh. You speak Greek, do you?

SERVANT. Yes, master.

CLEITUS. Then I suppose I'll have to kill you.

SERVANT. Why, master?

CLEITUS. You might be a spy——

SERVANT. If I were a spy I would not tell you I spoke Greek.

CLEITUS. There's sense in that, I suppose. What's your name?

SERVANT. Mazares.

CLEITUS. What outlandish names you barbarians do have. [CLEITUS *drains his wine, and then finds a place in his already bulging tunic for the cup.*] That you haven't seen—do you hear? Or I will kill you.

SERVANT. I haven't seen anything, master.

From outside the tent we hear the voice of PARMENION.

PARMENION [*off*]. Why are you guarding this tent?

SOLDIER [*off*]. Orders, sir.

PARMENION [*off*]. All right, let me through.

CLEITUS *mutters a curse.*

SOLDIER [*off*]. Sorry, sir.

PHILOTAS [*off*]. Damn it, man, don't you know the Chief of General Staff yet? This is General Parmenion.

PARMENION *appears inside the tent, followed by* PHILOTAS. *Both bear signs of battle.* CLEITUS *rises hurriedly to attention.* PARMENION *is an imposing-looking old soldier in the early sixties.*

PARMENION. Cleitus——

CLEITUS. Sir?

PARMENION. What are you doing here?

CLEITUS. Guarding the tent, sir.

PARMENION [*looking round*]. Hm. These were Darius' own quarters, I suppose.

CLEITUS. Yes, sir. I thought I'd better put a guard on them until the King got here. I didn't want anything touched.

PARMENION [*looking at him quizzically*]. No. Quite right. Any documents?

CLEITUS. I—er—haven't had time to look yet. [*A golden plate clatters to the floor, through his tunic.* CLEITUS *stoops to pick it up.* PARMENION *stops him, picks it up and hands it back to him*]. [*Confused*]. A little souvenir, sir. I thought I'd send it home to my wife. It has Darius' arms on it——

PARMENION. Indeed. That should certainly interest her very much.

PHILOTAS [*who has been wandering round the tent awestruck*]. God, but Darius knew how to live! Father—have you ever seen anything like this in all your life?

PARMENION [*looking round, gravely*]. No, my son. I can't say that I have. Not exactly the style of living one would expect of a commander-in-chief in the field.

CLEITUS [*virtuously*]. I agree. Disgusting, I call it.

PHILOTAS. Disgusting. I call it magnificent.

CLEITUS. You *would.*

PARMENION [*looking at servant*]. Who is this man?

CLEITUS. Darius' personal servant, sir. I found him hiding under the bed in there. [*He points to the connecting aperture.*] I gather there were a score or so of others, but some of the men got here first——

PARMENION. Killed? [CLEITUS *nods.*] A pity. They'd have been useful for interrogation. He speak Greek?

CLEITUS. Yes, sir.

PARMENION [*to* SERVANT]. Where are King Darius' documents?

SERVANT [*placidly*]. Burnt, master.

PARMENION. Burnt? Who burnt them?

SERVANT. I burnt them, master.

CLEITUS *draws his sword.*

CLEITUS. What? You treacherous hound! And I saved your life. [*He raises his sword.*]

PARMENION [*interposing*]. All right, Cleitus. He can still be useful. What's in that chest over there?

SERVANT. Would you like to open it, master?

PARMENION. Yes.

MAZARES *hands key to* PARMENION, *who throws it to* PHILOTAS, *who goes to chest and opens it.*

PARMENION. And then wait in there till we call for you.

He points to the sleeping quarters. MAZARES *goes out.* PARMENION *goes to chest.* PHILOTAS *emits a low whistle.*

PHILOTAS. Ye gods!

PARMENION [*at length*]. Well, gentlemen—it looks as if there'll be a chance at last to settle some arrears of pay——

PHILOTAS. Obliging of Darius—I must say.

PARMENION. If there's this much bullion here imagine what there is at Damascus—his forward base——

CLEITUS. God! The wealth of these barbarians! It makes one vomit.

PHILOTAS. Not me, it doesn't.

PARMENION [*pointing*]. What do you suppose those things were for? Presents?

CLEITUS. Perhaps decorations for gallantry.

PHILOTAS [*with a scornful laugh*]. Well, they'd hardly have been needed today.

CLEITUS. Oh, I don't know. They didn't fight too badly—for Persians.

PHILOTAS. Really? You consider they were beaten by sheer weight of numbers, then?

CLEITUS. There's no need to get sarcastic, young Philotas, just because you and your scented young cavalrymen went careering into a lot of raw conscripts who were already in full retreat. If you'd seen what happened to the Phalanx——

PHILOTAS [*easily*]. It was rather difficult to do that, wasn't it? I must say, for heavy armed troops I never saw such a fine burst of speed. One minute they were there, and the next minute they weren't. It was most spectacular——

CLEITUS. Are you insinuating that the Phalanx ran?

PARMENION [*pacifically*]. Now, gentlemen. We've fought one battle today——

CLEITUS. Yes, sir—but he insinuated the Phalanx ran——

PHILOTAS. Not ran. Decidedly not ran. Shall we say they were whisked backwards out of the battle by the Goddess Hera. She's always so kind to the infantry, I notice——

CLEITUS' *hand goes to his sword.* PARMENION *restrains him.*

PARMENION [*sharply*]. Stop it, Cleitus. He's only joking. I know what happened. The second division of the Phalanx, fighting a holding action, executed a brilliant tactical retreat. It wasn't your part of the line, anyway. Your division tore a vital gap in the enemy defences and the rest of the Phalanx went through. As for the cavalry action it did exactly what was planned—namely, to encircle and fold up the enemy's left wing. You people only see what's happening on your own sector. You can't possibly get the whole picture. It was a beautiful plan of battle and unlike most plans of battle, it worked perfectly in practice. You see, gentlemen, we all of us happen to have the honour of serving under a military genius.

PHILOTAS. Genius, father?

PARMENION. Yes, my son—that's what I said. And I know military genius when I see it. Don't forget I served under his father——

PHILOTAS. My estimate of Alexander as commander-in-chief is that he's a goodish cavalry captain with the devil's own luck.

CLEITUS. Sir—after insulting me, are you going to allow him to insult the King?

PHILOTAS [*hotly*]. Insult the King, you old blockhead? As if I would. I'm far closer to him than you are——

CLEITUS. That's a lie——

PHILOTAS. Oh yes, I know. You carried him in your arms as a child and saved his life at the Granicus, and he loves you as a father. I suppose we're going to hear all that again——

CLEITUS [*hand on sword again, to* PARMENION]. Sir—I *must* answer this. [*To* PILOTAS] Come outside.

PARMENION. Don't be a fool, Cleitus. [*To* PHILOTAS]. That tongue of yours will get you into trouble one of these days.

PHILOTAS. No doubt, father. A truthful tongue often does.

PARMENION. I've a good mind to order you to be confined to your quarters till further notice.

PHILOTAS. I wish you would, father. You don't know what's waiting for me in my quarters——

PARMENION. What?

PHILOTAS. Oh, a little package I had sent there half an hour ago.

PARMENION. A live package, I suppose?

PHILOTAS. And kicking.

PARMENION. You ought to be ashamed of yourself, sir.

PHILOTAS. Oh, I will be tomorrow, father, I'm sure I will. However, if I sacrifice handsomely to the Goddess of Virtue, doubtless my sin will be forgiven me.

PARMENION. Why was I cursed with such a son?

PHILOTAS. Isn't it rather strange of the Persians to bring their women to war with them?

PARMENION. They've always done it. Very bad for morale.

PHILOTAS. Bad for theirs, perhaps, but pretty good for ours.

There is another outburst of noise from the camp outside.

PARMENION. I don't agree with you. In fact I've half a mind to order the men back to our camp at once——

PHILOTAS. If you did you'd have a mutiny. Ask Cleitus. He'd be among the first to disobey that order.

CLEITUS. What do you mean by that?

PHILOTAS. You know perfectly well what I mean. I saw you you wicked old man—and what's more, I saw where you put them.

PARMENION. Them?

PHILOTAS. Three.

PARMENION. Three? Cleitus!

PHILOTAS. In a tent out there, guarded by his own Phalanxmen. Which reminds me, Cleitus, you'd better watch out. You know what your Phalanxmen are.

CLEITUS [*with dignity*]. Sir—the females to whom your son is referring happen to be three rather important prisoners whom I thought it best to have guarded until the King can see them himself.

PHILOTAS. Father Cleitus! You old rogue! Reserved for our ascetic monarch? You might have thought up something better than that.

CLEITUS [*To* PARMENION, *still with dignity*]. As you see, sir, I am under acute provocation from your son, but I can assure you my story is nevertheless accurate.

PARMENION. I don't doubt it, Cleitus. I don't doubt it. Who are these prisoners?

CLEITUS. With your permission, sir, I would rather tell His Majesty of that myself.

PARMENION. Quite so. I understand. [PHILOTAS *winks at his father, who conceals a smile. Evidently he does not believe him.*] [*Turning to the table.*] Well, as we're here, let's celebrate our Greek victory in some Persian wine.

CLEITUS. It's not at all bad, as a matter of fact, sir. Er—while waiting I did allow myself a sip.

PHILOTAS. Of course you did, Cleitus. You must have been so hot from your exertions in the battle.

CLEITUS. What's that!

PARMENION [*warningly*]. Now, now, gentlemen!

He has poured three cups.

PARMENION [*raising his cup*]. The King! [*They all drink.*]

PHILOTAS. Now I'll give you one. Ourselves! [*They drink again.*] After all, it's not every day that one helps to conquer half the world.

PARMENION. We haven't conquered anything today except a breathing space.

PHILOTAS. What? With sixty or seventy thousand dead and prisoners pouring in——

PARMENION. Half got away. And Darius still lives.

CLEITUS. Unless Alexander caught him up.

PARMENION. He hadn't a chance. Did you see that defile at the end? It was choked with men and animals, and Darius had a clear start. No human being could have ridden through that mess.

CLEITUS [*with fatherly pride*]. Alexander might.

PHILOTAS [*quietly*]. The God, Alexander?

CLEITUS [*also quietly*]. No. Just Alexander.

PHILOTAS. It's good stuff, this wine. These Persians certainly know how to live.

There is the sound of cheering.

PARMENION. Thank Heaven! That sounds as if he's back.

PHILOTAS. With Darius captive, do you think?

CLEITUS [*defiantly*]. Yes. I do.

The cheering has come close to the tent and now suddenly stops. ALEXANDER *comes in, followed by* HEPHAESTION. *He wears his battle armour, and has on his head the helmet with the conspicuous white plumes that he always sports in battle. He is limping heavily from a wound in the thigh.* HEPHAESTION *also shows the signs of battle. He carries a large bow and a purple mantle.* ALEXANDER *looks slowly round the tent, while the others watch him.*

ALEXANDER [*at length, murmuring*]. So this is what it is to be a king. [*He smiles slightly, then limps forward to the three men.*] Parmenion—Philotas—you've forestalled me, I see. [*He clasps hands with both of them.*] You did wonders—both of you——

PARMENION. Are you hurt, sir?

ALEXANDER. It's nothing. [*Seeing* CLEITUS.] Father Cleitus! [*He embraces him, laughing.*] You're safe, thank God! There was a rumour you were killed——

CLEITUS. It would take more than a rumour to kill me.

ALEXANDER. I knew it wasn't true. Even the Persians wouldn't have the heart to take Father Cleitus from me.

CLEITUS [*anxiously*]. Let's see that wound. [*He bends down to examine it.*]

ALEXANDER. Don't fuss, Father Cleitus. Hephaestion—show them what you're holding.

HEPHAESTION *displays his trophies.*

CLEITUS [*looking at the wound*]. This ought to be dressed.

ALEXANDER. In a minute.

CLEITUS [*severely*]. Now. [*Shouting.*] Here! You! What's-your-name! [MAZARES *appears.*] Bring a basin of water and a bandage.

MAZARES *bows and goes back into the sleeping quarters.*

ALEXANDER [*pointing to the trophies*]. Gentlemen, you are now looking at the bow and the mantle of Darius.

CLEITUS [*quickly*]. You've got him?

ALEXANDER. No. There wasn't a chance. But I found his chariot abandoned in a ditch. He must have got away on horseback. What do you think of the mantle?

HEPHAESTION [*to* ALEXANDER]. Try it on.

He throws it round his shoulders.

ALEXANDER. How does it suit me?

PHILOTAS [*with a faint edge to his voice*]. It might have been made for you.

MAZARES *comes out with the water and bandages. The water is in a carved gold bowl.*

MAZARES. The water, master.

CLEITUS *takes it.* MAZARES *retires.*

ALEXANDER. Let's see that. [*He takes the bowl from the hands of the kneeling* CLEITUS.] I admire his Persian Majesty's taste in camp furniture.

ALEXANDER *hands the bowl back to* CLEITUS *who begins to dress the wound.*

PARMENION [*pointing to the chest*]. There is another item of camp furniture over there that I think you will admire even more.

ALEXANDER. Let's see.

He limps over to the chest, to CLEITUS' *exasperation, as he has to follow him on his knees.* PHILOTAS *opens it.*

ALEXANDER [*peering inside*]. Useful. How much? Enough for arrears?

PARMENION. More than enough.

ALEXANDER. Give every man a bonus then.

PARMENION. But surely, sir, that would be very unwise. We must keep a reserve.

ALEXANDER. A reserve? Whatever for?

PARMENION. For the future.

ALEXANDER. The future will provide for itself. Philotas, have this chest taken back to camp under guard—and organise pay parades.

PHILOTAS. Tonight?

ALEXANDER. As soon as possible. I think you'll find it an effective way of getting the men back to camp.

PHILOTAS. Very effective, I should think. [*Calling.*] Hey, you two! [*Two* SOLDIERS *come in.*] Take this chest. [*To* ALEXANDER.] Shouldn't you count it first? [*As* ALEXANDER *opens his mouth.*] Please don't say whatever for, or I might have to tell you.

ALEXANDER. That's all right, Philotas. You can take what you like——

PHILOTAS. Oh God! Now, of course, I can't touch a thing. [*To* SOLDIERS.] All right, you two. Forward march.

He follows the two SOLDIERS *out.*

CLEITUS [*finishing his bandage*]. You're mad, Alexander. Clean off your head.

ALEXANDER. So many people think. [*Looking at bandage.*] Thank you, Father Cleitus. You're an expert nurse.

CLEITUS. You'd better let me look at it again tomorrow.

ALEXANDER. Perhaps.

CLEITUS. No perhaps about it. You'll do what I say. Now, I've got a little surprise for you.

ALEXANDER. What is it?

CLEITUS. You'll see in a minute. You wait there now. I won't be a second.

He goes out.

ALEXANDER [*To* PARMENION]. What's his surprise?

PARMENION. I gather it's a special reserve of female captives.

ALEXANDER. Oh God! Isn't that typical of Father Cleitus? Why do so many of my men expect me to behave like an animal?

PARMENION. Because most of your men behave like animals themselves.

ALEXANDER. I agree. You know—Parmenion—sex and sleep are the two things in this world that make me most conscious of my mortality.

PARMENION. Is that why you so persistently avoid both?

ALEXANDER. I suppose so.

PARMENION. You didn't sleep last night at all.

ALEXANDER. Hephaestion—have I ever—before a battle?

HEPHAESTION. Never.

PARMENION. At least you'll sleep tonight.

ALEXANDER. Perhaps. Parmenion—from the bottom of my heart—I thank you.

PARMENION. Thank me, sir? What for?

ALEXANDER. For winning my battle for me.

PARMENION. That isn't true.

ALEXANDER. Isn't it? Perhaps it isn't. I don't know. Anyway, we won it, and I thank you.

PARMENION. Thank the Gods, sir—not me.

ALEXANDER. I thank both. Parmenion, did my father ever thank you after his battles?

PARMENION [*uncomfortably*]. Yes, sir. Sometimes.

ALEXANDER. When he wasn't too drunk to remember, I suppose. What do you think he'd have felt if he'd been here today?

PARMENION. Very proud of his son.

Pause. ALEXANDER *laughs.*

ALEXANDER. You never really knew him, did you, Parmenion?

PARMENION. As well as I've ever known anyone.

ALEXANDER. Just about as well as you know me—I would say. [*He smiles.*] Go and stop Cleitus making a fool of himself, will you?

PARMENION. Yes, sir, if I can find him.

ALEXANDER. And then come back to dinner—— [PARMENION *goes.* ALEXANDER *suddenly throws his head back, and his body grows tense and rigid.*] [*Through his teeth.*] Oh God—if there is any justice in heaven—let my father know what I have done today. Let him see me now—in Darius' tent, wearing Darius' mantle—and let his eyes burn with the sight.

He stays with his eyes closed for a moment, and then he turns with a smile to HEPHAESTION.

ALEXANDER. Hephaestion—do you ever think I'm mad?

HEPHAESTION [*quietly*]. Yes, Alexander. Sometimes.

ALEXANDER. So do I. Sometimes. Give me some wine.

HEPHAESTION [*pouring a cup*]. A rare request from you.

ALEXANDER. I'm thirsty. [*He takes a gulp.*] Ugh! What a horrible taste wine has! I don't know how people can drink it. What shall I send to my mother?

HEPHAESTION. That cloak.

ALEXANDER [*abruptly*]. No. I wouldn't part with it. [*Looking round.*] Something with the Royal arms on.

HEPHAESTION. I know what I'm sending home.

ALEXANDER. What?

HEPHAESTION. A lion cub.

ALEXANDER. A lion cub?

HEPHAESTION. Yes. With the most beautiful jewelled collar. I found it wandering round the camp. It's in my tent now—probably eating all my clothes. An attractive piece of loot, I must say.

ALEXANDER. I know. I'll send her that basin old Cleitus washed my scratch in. She'll find an historic association in that. [*He points to the throne.*] I suppose that was Darius' throne.

HEPHAESTION. Yes. Imposing, isn't it?

ALEXANDER. Very.

HEPHAESTION. Strange object to bring on active service.

ALEXANDER. The Master of the World must keep his state. I wonder where he is now?

HEPHAESTION. The Master of the World? Hiding in a ditch somewhere, I expect.

ALEXANDER [*murmuring*]. How can a man become a god? Do you remember Aristotle's answer?

HEPHAESTION. By doing what is impossible for a man to do.

ALEXANDER. To lead thirty-five thousand against a quarter of a million and win—have I done the impossible, Hephaestion?

HEPHAESTION [*with a mock obeisance*]. Your divinity is assured, your translation in a fiery chariot imminent. I only hope you don't find it too cold for you on Olympus.

ALEXANDER [*musingly*]. Cold and lonely, perhaps.

HEPHAESTION [*still joking*]. Oh no. Surely not lonely—on Olympus.

ALEXANDER. Not on Olympus. On earth, I meant. [*He is staring at the throne.* HEPHAESTION'S *smile fades as he watches him.*] The true emperor is a god among men.

HEPHAESTION [*uncomfortably*]. You seem to have a memory for your tutor's precepts tonight.

ALEXANDER. I never forget them. [*Nodding towards the throne.*] That seat must be a very lonely place.

HEPHAESTION. It needn't be.

ALEXANDER. It must be.

HEPHAESTION. Then why—knowing that—should a man want to sit in it?

ALEXANDER. A difficult question to answer, Hephaestion. Perhaps it's because a man can beat every enemy in the world except his own destiny. [*Thoughtfully.*] If today I had killed Darius—[*after a pause, with a change of tone*] How near him did we come?

HEPHAESTION. About twenty paces——

ALEXANDER. Twenty paces from the empire of the world? Well, well. Next time let's pray for better luck. Come and inspect the rest of our loot. Let's see what's in here.

He goes into the other part of the tent, followed by HEPHAESTION. *There is a pause and then* CLEITUS' *voice can be heard outside.*

CLEITUS. [*off*]. In here. That's right. Stop wailing, you brat—or I'll give you something to wail about.

The QUEEN-MOTHER, *the* QUEEN *and the* PRINCESS ROYAL OF

PERSIA *come in one by one. The* PRINCESS *has been weeping, but* CLEITUS' *last threat has automatically silenced her. The* QUEEN-MOTHER *and the* QUEEN *are impassive. They keep their eyes firmly on the ground.* CLEITUS *has followed them in.*

CLEITUS. All right, now. Stand here. [*He pushes them roughly to face the sleeping quarters.*] Now. Kneel down. [*They kneel.*] That's right. [*He goes to the sleeping quarters' aperture.*] Your Majesty!

ALEXANDER [*off*]. Yes? What is it?

CLEITUS. Certain prisoners await Your Majesty's pleasure.

ALEXANDER *appears at the aperture.* HEPHAESTION *behind him.*

ALEXANDER [*angrily*]. Cleitus—you clown! I sent Parmenion to stop you——

CLEITUS. Did you? Well, I wasn't to be stopped anyway. [*He chuckles.*] How do you like 'em—eh?

ALEXANDER. Very much, but please take them away.

CLEITUS. Don't you want to ask them their names?

ALEXANDER. I don't want to know their names. [*To the women.*] Please don't kneel. Stand up. [*The* WOMEN *stand—the two older* WOMEN *still looking at the floor. But the* PRINCESS *looks at* ALEXANDER.] Cleitus—get them out of here. [*He turns to go back.*]

PRINCESS [*with a sudden cry.*] Mother—he's wearing father's cloak.

ALEXANDER, *his back to the three* WOMEN, *stands rooted for a second, then he turns slowly. The* QUEEN-MOTHER *raises her head and covers her face with her hands.*

ALEXANDER [*harshly*]. Cleitus—you're under arrest.

CLEITUS. Sir——

ALEXANDER. You are under arrest. How dare you do this. I'll never forgive you. Never.

CLEITUS. But—but—I thought you'd be pleased. I don't see the harm——

ALEXANDER. Get out, you barbarian! Get out! And count yourself lucky to leave this tent alive. [CLEITUS, *too aggrieved for words, salutes and leaves.* ALEXANDER *approaches the three* WOMEN.] If there is anything in the world I can do to wipe out this insult, you must tell me and it shall be done.

QUEEN-MOTHER [*in a dead voice*]. There is no insult. We are your prisoners, and you may do to us as you please.

ALEXANDER. You are the Queen-Mother of Persia?

QUEEN-MOTHER. I am.

ALEXANDER. Your son is not dead. Nor is he captured. [*The* QUEEN-MOTHER *bites her hand to repress a cry.*] He fought as bravely as a man can fight. The Gods were not on his side—that is all.

QUEEN-MOTHER. He is safe, then?

ALEXANDER. Yes, madam. He lives to fight again. Hephaestion?

HEPHAESTION [*stepping forward*]. Sir.

ALEXANDER. I am placing these ladies in your charge. [*To* QUEEN-MOTHER.] Where are your proper quarters?

QUEEN-MOTHER. They were in the two tents next to this.

ALEXANDER [*to* HEPHAESTION]. Escort them there. Put a guard of honour on duty. Find them servants and see that they are given every comfort that they are used to.

HEPHAESTION. Yes, sir.

ALEXANDER [*to* QUEEN-MOTHER]. You can go with him with an easy heart. He will see that you come to no harm. He is my closest friend and wisest counsellor.

QUEEN-MOTHER. We thank you, sir.

ALEXANDER. Before you go, is there anything that I myself can do for you?

The two older WOMEN *shake their heads softly. The* PRINCESS *speaks.*

PRINCESS. Yes, please. Can you find Marduk?

ALEXANDER. Who is Marduk?

PRINCESS. My lion cub. I think he's been stolen, because I heard him making a terrible noise.

ALEXANDER *exchanges a glance with* HEPHAESTION.

ALEXANDER. Yes. I think I can find Marduk for you. What is more, I think I can find the thief. If I do, what would you like done to him?

PRINCESS [*after due thought*]. Put him in Marduk's cage.

ALEXANDER. An excellent idea. Hephaestion—see that order carried out.

HEPHAESTION [*gloomily*]. Yes, sir.

ALEXANDER. Goodnight, then. With your permission I shall call upon you tomorrow to see that you are comfortable.

QUEEN-MOTHER. You will be very welcome. [*The three women follow* HEPHAESTION *to the entrance. The* QUEEN-MOTHER *turns back.*]

It is wrong of me to ask, sir, I know—but my son—you are not lying to save our feelings? Is he really alive and safe?

ALEXANDER. I can assure you of that, madam. I saw him escape myself.

QUEEN-MOTHER. Escape?

ALEXANDER. In that part of the field—he was outnumbered.

QUEEN-MOTHER. I see. Thank you, sir.

She turns to follow the others.

ALEXANDER. Your Majesty.

ALEXANDER, *with a sudden gesture, takes off Darius' mantle and places it over her shoulders.*

ALEXANDER. In case you feel cold in the night. [*The* QUEEN-MOTHER, *her back to* ALEXANDER, *covers her face with a sudden gesture. Her shoulders shake for a second, but no sound comes from her mouth. Then she straightens her shoulders and follows the others out, holding* DARIUS' *cloak closely to her.*] [*Calling, after a pause.*] Here. You in there! Get that bath ready for me!

MAZARES [*off*]. Yes, master.

ALEXANDER *wanders to the table and eats a mouthful of food. He thrusts aside the plate he is eating from and gets up. He stares for some time at the throne. Then, slowly and resolutely, he climbs the few steps and seats himself in it, running his hands along its arms.* MAZARES *comes in, and advances towards* ALEXANDER. *A few steps away he stops, kneels down, and places his forehead to the floor.* HEPHAESTION *appears at the entrance, unnoticed by* ALEXANDER.]

ALEXANDER [*quietly*]. Yes?

MAZARES. All is in readiness for your Imperial Majesty.

ALEXANDER *nods. The* SERVANT *rises and backs slowly out, bowing very low as he reaches the exit.* ALEXANDER *stares after him thoughtfully. Then, in turning his head slightly he catches sight of* HEPHAESTION, *who is watching him with a cool, steady gaze. He smiles.* HEPHAESTION *does not answer it. Then he jumps down from the throne.*

ALEXANDER. Come and watch me take my imperial bath.

HEPHAESTION *does not move.*

THE LIGHTS FADE

SCENE FOUR

The gardens at Babylon. DARIUS *is on the seat where we last saw him and* BESSUS *sits on the bench.* PALACE OFFICIAL *is kneeling before* DARIUS.

PALACE OFFICIAL. The envoy of the King of Macedon awaits your pleasure.

DARIUS. Let him approach.

The OFFICIAL *rises, bows and goes.*

BESSUS. You shouldn't receive him here. You should receive him in the throne room—in state.

DARIUS [*wearily*]. I am tired of state.

BESSUS. At least you should have had yourself announced by your titles.

DARIUS. My titles are not very likely to impress the envoy of the man who is already usurping most of them.

BESSUS. All the more reason to give yourself your rightful style.

DARIUS [*bitterly*]. Is—"Master of the World" still my rightful style?

BESSUS. Certainly.

DARIUS. With my wife, my daughter and my mother in another's power?

BESSUS. They will be returned to you soon.

DARIUS. At the price of nearly half that world of which you say I am still the master.

BESSUS. The offer was far too generous, sir. If you remember I spoke against it in the Council ...

DARIUS [*bitterly*]. Yes, you did, Bessus. You did. But then, you see, it was not your family who were captive. [*The* OFFICIAL *returns with* PHILOTAS—*a very resplendent* PHILOTAS—*glittering with jewels and decorations. He looks at* DARIUS *with interest but barely glances at* BESSUS. *He does not bow to either. The* OFFICIAL *goes out.*] You are welcome to Babylon, sir. You had, I trust, a pleasant journey.

PHILOTAS. Thank you. Most comfortable.

DARIUS. You arrived last night, I understand.

PHILOTAS. That is so.

DARIUS. You came direct from Egypt?

PHILOTAS. In eleven days.

DARIUS. You travelled very fast. Your King is in Memphis?

PHILOTAS. In Alexandria.

DARIUS. Alexandria?

PHILOTAS [*carelessly*]. A city we are building near the Nile delta. It's going to be the greatest port in the world. I should have thought you'd have heard of it.

DARIUS. No. [*With a smile.*] My spies seem to have been very lax. Where is the exact site?

PHILOTAS. Do you know Egypt?

BESSUS [*angrily*]. You are speaking, sir, to the Pharaoh of Egypt.

PHILOTAS. Oh yes, of course. That was one of your titles, wasn't it?

DARIUS [*gently*]. Yes, it was. Where is the site?

PHILOTAS. Between Lake Mareotis and the sea.

DARIUS. An admirable choice. Strangely enough I had myself thought of founding a sea-port there. I would have called it Dareia. Well now, sir—I won't detain you any longer. No doubt, before our conference tomorrow, you have many matters to talk over with your staff——

PHILOTAS. My staff? I haven't any staff.

DARIUS. Are you alone?

PHILOTAS. Of course.

DARIUS. But these negotiations—involving as they do the question of boundaries—may be very complicated. Are you sure——

PHILOTAS. Quite sure. And I don't think the negotiations will turn out to be nearly as complicated as you think.

Pause. DARIUS *and* BESSUS *exchange a glance.*

DARIUS. I see.

PHILOTAS. What's more, I have to start back for Egypt tomorrow at first light. So I think, with your permission, I shall come to business straight away.

DARIUS. You have my permission.

PHILOTAS [*with an ironical bow*]. Thank you. King Alexander replies to your tenders of peace in the following way. Regarding the ransom of ten thousand talents which you offer for your family, he says that he is in no immediate need of money, and if he were he would find other means of acquiring it.

BESSUS. By robbery?

PHILOTAS. By conquest.

DARIUS. Go on.

PHILOTAS. Regarding the suggestion you make of a possible future marriage between your daughter and himself he thanks you, but asks me to state that should he ever consider making such a match it will certainly not occur to him to ask his father-in-law's consent.

BESSUS. By God, you're a brave man to come here on such a mission!

DARIUS. Silence, Bessus. Go on, sir.

PHILOTAS. Finally, regarding your offer of Egypt, Asia Minor and the lands west of the Euphrates, he thanks you again, but finds it hard to understand why you should have troubled yourself to give him what is already his. Should you, on the other hand, wish to offer him the lands of the Persian Empire east of the Euphrates, he will accept. In addition, he would ask you to surrender your person to him, and desires me to assure you that no harm will come to you should you do so. On any terms other than those war between you must continue.

DARIUS. He is demanding that I surrender my empire without condition?

PHILOTAS. The condition is that you yourself will come to no harm.

DARIUS. Go to that parapet, sir, and look down at the plain. [PHILOTAS *does so.*] What do you see?

PHILOTAS. An army camp.

DARIUS. The size of it doesn't impress you?

PHILOTAS. Mere size very rarely does.

DARIUS. I have over half a million men under arms. They have been in training all the winter. More are joining the colours every day. Does your King really believe that if he crosses the Euphrates into the heart of this great continent, thousands of miles from his base, and meets such an army on the great plains of Babylon—for you may be sure I shall not repeat my mistake at Issus and fight in the mountains—does your King really believe that then he would have more than one chance in a million of getting back to Greece alive?

PHILOTAS. Evidently he must, or I would hardly have been commissioned to bring you this message. And what message shall I take back to him?

DARIUS. You may tell him this. My offer to him was fair, sincere and generous. I made it for one reason only—because he holds in his possession the three people who are dearest to me in all the world, and without whom I cannot live. For their sake I was prepared to betray my country and make a dishonourable peace. Now he has relieved me of the choice and I feel strangely glad that in doing so he has recalled me to my duty. I shall fight Alexander without mercy for him or thought for my family. And of course I shall win, for it cannot be otherwise. My chamberlain will escort you back to your quarters.

PHILOTAS. One moment, sir—before I leave. I have a very painful duty to perform. An unofficial duty—but I mustn't shirk it. I have some news now that I must tell you——

DARIUS. Yes?

PHILOTAS. Your wife—you had heard she wasn't well——

DARIUS. I had heard.

PHILOTAS. I'm afraid she—everything that could possibly be done for her was done—but she didn't seem to recover as she should—just a fever, that was all—it wasn't the doctor's fault. They say she didn't want to live——[*Pause.*]

DARIUS [*at length*]. I see.

PHILOTAS. I'm sorry. I should have broken the news less clumsily. I'm not really used to these diplomatic missions. [DARIUS *says nothing.*] [*Repeating words learnt parrot-fashion*] I am commanded by His Majesty to express his deepest sympathy for you in your irreparable loss.

DARIUS [*in a whisper*]. You must thank His Majesty for me.

PHILOTAS. I will. Here are some private letters for you.

He hands BESSUS *some letters and goes out. There is a pause* DARIUS *has not moved.*

BESSUS [*handing letters to* DARIUS]. I need hardly tell you, sir, what I feel for you at this moment.

DARIUS. Thank you, Bessus. Call the Council for tonight. I shall decree general mobilisation.

BESSUS. Yes, sir.

DARIUS. And training must be intensified. We have six months before he can cross the desert. This time we'll take no chances. Alexander must be killed.

BESSUS. Yes, we need that head to decorate your palace gate.

There is a pause while DARIUS *reads his letter.*

DARIUS. Listen to this, Bessus. It's from my daughter—— [*Reading.*] "The funeral was very sad for grandmother and me. Mother was given all the royal honours. Alexander was there and he was crying dreadfully. Afterwards he came home with us and played games to cheer me up; and then he came every day after that for a week with a different present for me every time. He is so gentle and kind—not a bit like a soldier. I wish he wasn't your enemy. Otherwise you would love him, I know, as grandmother and I do——" [*He stares at* BESSUS.] [*Murmuring.*] What kind of a man are we fighting?

BESSUS [*with an indifferent shrug*]. A madman.

DARIUS. There is a devil in him. I know that.

BESSUS. A devil that's mercifully leading him to his own destruction.

DARIUS. To his or to ours?

BESSUS. To both, perhaps. But certainly to his. [*He gets up and bows.*] I'll summon the Council of War.

He goes out.

DARIUS *continues staring into space.*

THE LIGHTS FADE

SCENE FIVE

Alexander's tent. This is the same tent that Alexander captured at Issus and which ever since he has used for himself. The furnishings, however, have been considerably changed. A long bare table replaces the sumptuous Persian one, and the gold and silver decorations have been removed. It is night, and the tent is lit by lamps.

Present are PARMENION, PHILOTAS, CLEITUS, HEPHAESTION, PERDICCAS *and* PTOLEMY. *They are talking in low voices, grouped near the table.*

Their voices are hushed as ALEXANDER *enters, and comes to the head of the table.*

ALEXANDER. Are we all here?

PARMENION. All present, sir.

ALEXANDER. Sit down, please. [*They sit on stools round the table.*] Ptolemy, I've asked you to be present because if anything happens to me you will take over the special duties I have assigned to Parmenion, who, of course, will automatically assume the responsibility of Commander-in-Chief.

PTOLEMY. I understand.

They are now all seated. ALEXANDER *at the head of the table stands to address them.*

ALEXANDER. Well, gentlemen, I don't think I need spend too much time on the general situation. You all know it pretty thoroughly. One mile away, in front of a village called Gaugemela, the enemy has deployed an army roughly twice the size of the one he brought against us at Issus. It might, of course, have been four times as large, if we had given him more time to prepare—but our crossing of the desert in summer has evidently been as much of a surprise to him as we'd hoped it would be. Nevertheless we are faced by a hostile army of nearly half a million and there can be now no question—here in the heart of Asia—of retreat or of evading battle. Our objective is simple. We must destroy that army or that army will destroy us. [*The others nod approval.*] That is agreed? Good. Now the ground between our two armies has been well reconnoitred. You were right, Perdiccas. It has been tampered with.

PERDICCAS. They've dug concealed pits?

ALEXANDER. No; the exact reverse. They have carefully levelled a corridor about five hundred paces wide. And that shows us their main battle plan—to use their heavy scythed chariots in a charge against our right centre—presumably at the hinge between the sixth division of the Phalanx and the first division of the horse guards. At least—if I were Darius that is where I would try to make the break through. Now gentlemen. In view therefore of what I've seen today I am adopting the second of the two alternative plans I gave you yesterday. That is to say we are going to rely on the enemy's lack of cohesion in battle. Just to remind you of the general outline—you have the details—we are going to let the enemy outflank us on both wings. In fact, on this plain, and with his vast numbers we can hardly prevent him. We are therefore drawing up in a hollow square—not complete, until necessity arises, and the enemy reaches our rear. Then I shall use Darius' own tactics against him, and launch the entire Companion cavalry straight at the hinge in his line, force a break through and turn inwards against the centre, where Darius will be himself. Our objective will be the death, capture or flight of the enemy Commander-in-Chief. Are there any comments?

Pause. After a moment's hesitation PARMENION *rises.*

PARMENION. Might I speak, sir?

ALEXANDER. Of course.

PARMENION. I am not going to criticise your plan. Against an enemy outnumbering us by more than ten to one, it is, I think, the best that can be devised. But I would like to suggest another.

ALEXANDER. Yes. What is it?

PARMENION. A surprise attack by night.

There is a pause, while ALEXANDER *looks at him steadily.*

ALEXANDER [*at length*]. I will not steal a victory. Are there any other comments? [*He looks round the table. All shake their heads.*] Very well, gentlemen. You had better all go to your various headquarters and issue your orders for tomorrow. See that the men are served a hot meal one hour before dawn. We move at first light. They must get as much rest as they can, so see to it that there is only a bare minimum of fatigues and sentry duties. One thing is very certain. The Persians won't attack at night.

PHILOTAS. Might it be an idea to take a couple of patrols out to the Persian lines? I could easily organise a bit of a panic out there—using very few men—and making the devil of a lot of noise. Good idea if we could keep them standing to all night, don't you think? The poor bastards will probably fall asleep on the battlefield tomorrow.

ALEXANDER. Yes, Philotas. Organise that, but don't go yourself.

PHILOTAS [*disappointed*]. Yes. But, sir——

ALEXANDER. I don't want *you* a casualty before the battle.

PHILOTAS [*aggrieved*]. I wouldn't have suggested it if I thought you'd do that to me.

ALEXANDER *laughs, and then turns to the others who are making for the opening of the tent.*

ALEXANDER. One word more. This is our last battle. If we win it—the world is ours. If we lose it, we are dead. I think that's all that needs to be said. Goodnight, gentlemen, and a pleasant rest till dawn. PARMENION, PERDICCAS, PHILOTAS *and* HEPHAESTION *murmur goodnight and begin to file out.*] Hephaestion? [HEPHAESTION *detaches himself from the others.*] [*Smiling.*] Are you prepared for another all-night vigil?

HEPHAESTION. Of course.

ALEXANDER. I wonder how many hours of sleep I must have robbed you of in your life, Hephaestion?

HEPHAESTION [*simply*]. You've robbed me of nothing, Alexander. If you're awake, why should I want to sleep?

ALEXANDER [*with a smile*]. Come back, then. I shall need you.

HEPHAESTION *nods and goes out, following the others.* CLEITUS *and* PTOLEMY *have stayed.*

CLEITUS. Mind you take proper care of yourself tomorrow, Alexander. Don't go charging chariots like you did at the Granicus.

ALEXANDER [*smiling*]. Because you won't be there to save my life—eh, Father Cleitus? Don't worry about me. I'll be all right.

CLEITUS. Oh, it's not you I'm worried about. It's us. If we lose you here in the middle of Asia I don't know how we'd ever find our way back to Greece again. You're the only one who seems to know it. Goodnight, sir.

ALEXANDER. Goodnight, father. You take care of *yourself.*

CLEITUS. I will—never fear.

CLEITUS *embraces him and goes out.*

PTOLEMY *comes up to* ALEXANDER.

PTOLEMY. Sir—we have to discuss the disposition of the Archer Brigade for tomorrow——

ALEXANDER. Later.

PTOLEMY. But, sir—this is urgent——

ALEXANDER. Later.

PTOLEMY. I must repeat, sir. Your decision on this matter cannot wait——

ALEXANDER. It must. For an hour or two, it must. But now I must be alone.

PTOLEMY. But, sir——

ALEXANDER. I tell you, Ptolemy, it must wait. Take a walk into the night and look at the stars. [*He leads him to the entrance.*] In this part of the world you see them very clearly. Or if you climb that mound over there you can see the Persian camp fires—only, unlike the stars, there are so many of them that they are hard to pick out one by one. Just a blur of light on the horizon. And if you listen very carefully you can hear the hum of their voices as they talk to each other in the night. One of my pages said it sounded like the distant roaring of the sea. An imaginative boy. Too imaginative to make a soldier. See that he's sent home, will you. His name is Eusthenes. Remember that, Eusthenes. Now go and come back later.

PTOLEMY *goes.* ALEXANDER *stands there quite still facing into the tent. He is shivering, and his hands begin to shake. He raises them to the level of his eyes and stares at them, fascinated.* MAZARES, *his servant, comes in, and makes him his usual obeisance.* ALEXANDER *quickly puts his hands under his arms.*

ALEXANDER. Yes?

MAZARES. Shall I prepare Your Majesty's bed?

ALEXANDER. No. I shall remain in here. [MAZARES *backs away and goes out.*] [*In a whisper.*] Why do my hands shake? God! God! Take this fear from me, What is it I fear? Is it wounding, capture, pain, death? I've never feared them before. Why do I fear them now? Is it the thought of losing my battle? But I can't lose it. I am invincible. What is it, then? Is it the thought of winning my battle? Is that it, God? If it is, then my fear is nothing. Tomorrow I am Master of the World—the mortal partner of the Gods. Or I am dead. Either way there is nothing to fear. So take this agony from me. [*His hands as he watches continue to shake.*] Father! Father Philip! I invoke you, then. Look down at me now and sneer. Say—"See what a weak effeminate coward I have for a son." Say that, father! You used to say it often enough in your lifetime. Say it now, and help me, for only anger can conquer fear. [*His hands gradually stop their shaking and remain motionless.*] You see? Thank you, dear father. I am grateful.

PARMENION *comes in.*

PARMENION. Sir——

ALEXANDER. I gave orders I was not to be disturbed——

PARMENION. I make no apology for that. I have two matters to tell you, and they both concern your life.

ALEXANDER [*not interested*]. Yes?

PARMENION. The first is this. Our agents report that Darius has formed a special detachment of his horse guards—the so-called Immortals—whose single aim in the battle tomorrow will be to cut through to wherever you may be and strike you down—at whatever cost to themselves. Each man has taken a separate vow to kill you or die.

ALEXANDER [*indifferently*]. Then I suppose they will die—which, for Immortals, should prove an interesting experience.

PARMENION. I must beg you to take the threat seriously, sir—and I'd suggest that tomorrow you neither wear your red cloak nor ride Bucephalus.

ALEXANDER. Why ever not?

PARMENION. Both make you so conspicuous.

ALEXANDER. Exactly.

PARMENION. If I might suggest, sir—perhaps someone else might——

ALEXANDER. Who, for instance?

PARMENION [*hesitantly*]. If I shaved my beard off——

ALEXANDER [*laughing*]. You'd still look forty years too old and much too ugly. Besides, dear old Bucephalus would never forgive me if I let someone else ride him into battle. No, Parmenion. I appreciate the offer—but I'll give the Immortals a fair view of their quarry tomorrow. I'll even shout to them "Here's Alexander, if you want him." What's the other thing?

PARMENION. It's more serious, sir. A plot on your life—here in this camp.

ALEXANDER. That's interesting. Go on.

PARMENION. This time it was a Persian spy whom we caught yesterday and who confessed to us under torture that the mission given him was to secure your death by poison.

ALEXANDER. Really? How was he going to do that?

PARMENION. Through an agent.

ALEXANDER. What agent?

PARMENION. The Queen-Mother of Persia.

ALEXANDER [*laughing*]. Poor man! A forlorn mission they gave him.

PARMENION [*brusquely*]. His mission was successful, sir. He was on his way back to the Persian lines when we caught him. The Queen-Mother had promised him she would do what he asked. [ALEXANDER *stares at him without speaking*.] I realise, of course, that this must come as a great shock to you. You have, I know, been on the friendliest possible terms with the lady and have behaved to her almost as though she were your own mother. But you must remember that she is a Persian and that you are her son's deadliest enemy. So you see——

ALEXANDER. How was it to be done?

PARMENION. I understand she is in the habit of mixing you some kind of a drink every evening, isn't she? [ALEXANDER *nods*.] You may have noticed she hasn't done so tonight.

ALEXANDER [*sharply*]. You haven't——

PARMENION. Oh no, sir. I've left her for you to deal with.

ALEXANDER. Have you said anything to her at all.

PARMENION. No, sir. I merely had a sentry prevent her from bringing you the drink a few minutes ago. I said you were still in council. She was angry, I may say. She said it would get cold.

ALEXANDER [*calling*]. Mazares! [MAZARES *appears*.] Tell the Queen-Mother that I am now ready for my drink.

MAZARES. Yes, master. [*He goes out.*]

PARMENION. I'm extremely sorry, sir. I know how upsetting——

ALEXANDER. All right, Parmenion. You did your duty. Leave me, will you?

PARMENION. Yes, sir. [*He pulls out a document.*] Here is a verbatim account of the interrogation if you wish to confront her with it——

ALEXANDER. Give it to me. Now go.

PARMENION *gives him the document.*

PARMENION. Perhaps as a precaution we might have the sentries inside the tent——

ALEXANDER. No. Goodnight, Parmenion—until dawn.

PARMENION. Until dawn. Goodnight, sir.

MAZARES *enters, followed by two soldiers who stand at the entrance.*

MAZARES. Her Majesty awaits your pleasure.

ALEXANDER. Let her pass the guards and have the curtains drawn. (MAZARES *signs to the guards to draw the curtains.* SOLDIERS *draw curtains and go. The* QUEEN-MOTHER *enters through curtains held back by* MAZARES. *He goes out.* ALEXANDER *picks up the report and begins to read it. The* QUEEN-MOTHER *comes in with a cup from which a little steam is rising.* ALEXANDER *smiles at her and takes the cup.*] It didn't get cold?

QUEEN-MOTHER. I kept it warm.

He sits down on the bed, with the drink in his hands.

ALEXANDER. Have you seen the Persian camp fires?

QUEEN-MOTHER. Yes.

ALEXANDER. A beautiful sight, isn't it?

QUEEN-MOTHER. Beautiful.

ALEXANDER. Come and sit by me, here, will you. [*He indicates a stool near the bed. She sits down. He takes from his tunic the report he has been reading.*] You read Greek, don't you?

QUEEN-MOTHER. Yes. You know I do.

ALEXANDER. Well, just read that, will you, to yourself, while I drink this.

She begins to read. ALEXANDER *watches her a second and then takes a deep draught of the drink. After reading a few lines she looks up at him, startled.* ALEXANDER *smiles at her, and takes another gulp, finishing the drink. He hands her back the cup, and lies back contentedly. The* QUEEN-MOTHER *gets up and puts the cup on the table. He watches her, smiling.*]

QUEEN-MOTHER. Alexander, that was a foolish thing to do.

ALEXANDER. Why?

QUEEN-MOTHER. This report might have been true.

ALEXANDER. I suppose it might.

QUEEN-MOTHER. You've no right to take risks like that.

ALEXANDER. Perhaps not. Did you see this man?

QUEEN-MOTHER. Yes.

ALEXANDER. Did he ask you to poison me?

QUEEN-MOTHER. Yes.

ALEXANDER. And you said you would?

QUEEN-MOTHER. If I hadn't he would have asked someone else. I'm not the only Persian in your camp.

Pause. ALEXANDER, *lying back, studies her.*

ALEXANDER [*gently*]. Why *didn't* you kill me? Tomorrow I'm going to try and kill your son.

She turns quickly away from him, with a sob.

QUEEN-MOTHER. Alexander——

ALEXANDER. Don't cry, please don't cry. It's I who want to cry tonight.

QUEEN-MOTHER. Why do you have to fight him, Alexander?

ALEXANDER. I don't know. If I knew I'd tell you. I only know I must.

QUEEN-MOTHER. He's only a mile away out there. I could go to him now—this minute—I could offer him peace——

ALEXANDER. He'd be a fool to accept it.

QUEEN-MOTHER. He would from me. I'll go, Alexander, so gladly—if you'll only let me.

ALEXANDER. No, mother, I won't let you.

QUEEN-MOTHER. [*in tears*]. He's a gentle, kind man, like you. What harm has he ever done you?

ALEXANDER. None.

QUEEN-MOTHER. Then why do you hate him?

ALEXANDER. I don't hate him. If he's anything like you, I think I might love him.

QUEEN-MOTHER. And yet you must try to kill him——

ALEXANDER. I must.

QUEEN-MOTHER. Oh, Alexander——

ALEXANDER. Don't cry. Please don't cry. [*She sits on the bed.*] My own mother is very far away, you know.

QUEEN-MOTHER. I know. Have you sent her a messenger today?

ALEXANDER. I didn't have time, but I shall send her one tomorrow. [*Repeating to himself.*] After tomorrow.

QUEEN-MOTHER. Try to get some rest now.

ALEXANDER [*after a pause*]. Did Darius hate his father?

QUEEN-MOTHER. No. He loved his father. Why? What made you think——

ALEXANDER. I was just wondering. When did he die?

QUEEN-MOTHER. It must be nearly twenty years ago now.

ALEXANDER. And did you love him too?

QUEEN-MOTHER. Yes. Very dearly.

ALEXANDER [*drowsily*]. Strange.

QUEEN-MOTHER. Why is it strange?

ALEXANDER. I don't know. [*He has closed his eyes and is near sleep. The* QUEEN-MOTHER *looks down at the head on her lap.*] [*Murmuring.*] Goodnight, mother.

QUEEN-MOTHER. Goodnight, my son.

She bends down and gently kisses his brow. HEPHAESTION *comes in and sits on the stool by the bed watching. Neither he nor the* QUEEN-MOTHER *moves.*

ALEXANDER [*murmuring*]. After tomorrow.

He turns his head over and settles himself to sleep.

CURTAIN

ACT II

SCENE ONE

The stage is dark, but we can dimly discern the outline of a small farm-cart, battered and broken down, and inside a figure, wrapped in a blanket.

BESSUS [*off*]. Darius, Darius. [A MAN, *dirty, dishevelled and ragged, comes on, and speaks with the voice of* BESSUS.] [*Shaking the man in the cart.*] Darius! Darius! Wake up. Wake up —for Heaven's sake! We must start at once. We haven't a moment to lose.

DARIUS [*whimpering*]. Water!

BESSUS *reluctantly slips a flask off his shoulder, unfastens it and hands it to him.*

BESSUS. Only a sip. It's precious. We'll have to ride through the day. [*He snatches the flask back.*] That's enough——

DARIUS [*weakly*]. Please——

BESSUS. No. We can't spare it. We must start. The horses are being saddled——

DARIUS. Prince Bessus—I command you. Water.

BESSUS. No. [*He takes the weakly moaning king by the shoulders.*] Listen, Darius. You must try to understand. Alexander is only an hour or two behind us——

DARIUS, *sitting in the cart, laughs weakly.*

BESSUS. Did you hear what I said, sir?

DARIUS. Yes. I heard.

BESSUS. I've just had word he left the road at the last village and is riding straight for us—the short way through the open desert.

DARIUS [*still laughing weakly*]. You said that wasn't possible.

BESSUS. I said that no man in his senses would try it.

DARIUS. And you remember what I said, Bessus. Do you remember what I said?

BESSUS [*impatiently*]. Yes, I remember. You were right, and I was wrong. Get up, sir—please. We must start.

DARIUS. I said he was neither a man—nor in his senses. A mad demi-god.

BESSUS. Get on your feet, sir.

He practically lifts him out of the cart, supporting him when he is on his feet.

DARIUS. Bessus—isn't it strange that—as he's a god—it should have taken him so long to catch us——

BESSUS. He hasn't caught us yet. And if we can get into the mountains of Bactria he never will—not if he's Zeus himself. Courage, sir. Courage.

DARIUS. How far to Bactria?

BESSUS. Something under eight hundred miles.

DARIUS. How short a way you make that sound!

BESSUS. We've already come twice that distance.

DARIUS. I had forgotten that my empire was so wide. Let me go back to my cart and sleep.

He half collapses in cart.

BESSUS [*savagely*]. Wake up! Wake up!

He hits DARIUS' *head with his open palm.*

DARIUS. Leave me, Bessus. Save yourself. Thank you for all you have done for me. I am truly grateful. One day, perhaps, I shall honour you for it. Leave me now. Let me sleep.

BESSUS [*desperately*]. Sir—your men are waiting for your orders.

DARIUS. My men? How many men have I this morning?

BESSUS. Three hundred.

DARIUS. Still three hundred? No more desertions? Three hundred is a large army. With it—if I were Alexander—I could conquer the world.

BESSUS. With it you—Darius—can still reconquer the world. Reach Bactria and you can have an army of many, many thousands——

BESSUS *stands away from* DARIUS, *who sinks weakly to his knees.* A SOLDIER *comes running on.*

SOLDIER [*gasping*]. Less than a mile away—riding straight for us——

BESSUS. How many?

SOLDIER. About fifty——

BESSUS. Is Alexander with them?

SOLDIER. A white horse and a red cloak——

BESSUS. The Gods have delivered him into our hands. He can't know our numbers. [*To* DARIUS.] Do you hear that, Darius? Alexander is riding straight for us. Fifty against three hundred. [*To* SOLDIER.] Get the men into battle formation.

SOLDIER. I've tried, sir. They're out of hand. Some have ridden off. The others want to surrender.

BESSUS. Darius! Darius! [DARIUS *has crawled back into the cart. He kneels up as* BESSUS *calls him.*] Come down to the lines. Order your men to fight. They will for you—shout from here, if you like. They can hear you. [*Shouting.*] Soldiers of Persia. Hear your King—Darius!

DARIUS [*on his feet*]. Soldiers of Persia—I, Darius, Great King of Persia and Lord of Asia, command you to lay down your arms and surrender yourselves to Alexander——

BESSUS *leaps at him with drawn sword, and runs him through.* DARIUS *falls back into the cart, moaning feebly.*

BESSUS. Where's my horse? Lead me——

SOLDIER [*horrified*]. The King——

BESSUS. I am your King. Lead me to my horse——

He runs out, followed by the SOLDIER.

DARIUS. Bessus! Bessus! Why am I alone? Come quickly, someone. Come quickly. The Master of the World is dying and he must name his successor. [*Plaintively.*] Where are my attendants? [*Calling.*] Mazares, where are you? Artobazus! Spitamenes! [*He claps his hands feebly.*] Come quick, or it will be too late. Someone must hear what I have to say. [*He claps his hands again.*] Is it nothing to any of you to whom I bequeath my empire? [*Shouting.*] Come to me, someone! Come to me!

A GREEK SOLDIER *comes on, with drawn sword.*

SOLDIER. Who are you?

DARIUS. The enemy. Come here, my friend, and listen. [*The* GREEK SOLDIER *approaches stealthily, his sword at the ready suspecting a trap.* DARIUS, *kneeling in the cart, grasps his arm.*] I am dying, and you must listen to what I have to say.

SOLDIER. I'm listening.

DARIUS. I, Darius, Great King of Persia—— [*The* SOLDIER *starts back.* DARIUS, *his support gone, topples back. Then he drags himself painfully up on to the rail of the cart.*] Do you still hear me, Greek? I, Darius, Great King of Persia, do hereby name as my lawful and true successor, Alexander of Macedon—and I do solemnly adjure him in my name——

He falters, gasps and suddenly falls across the rail, his head hanging down. The SOLDIER, *awed and terrified, approaches him cautiously. He lifts his head up and stares at it. Then he lets it drop and runs off.*

*There is a pause, and then the stage begins to fill with shadowy figures—*GREEK SOLDIERS, *followed by* ALEXANDER *and* HEPHAESTION. ALEXANDER *walks slowly forward, in silence and stares for some moments at the dead* DARIUS.

ALEXANDER [*to* SOLDIERS]. What are you all staring at? Have none of you ever seen a dead Persian before? [*The* SOLDIERS *drift away, still in silence.* ALEXANDER *and* HEPHAESTION *are left alone.*] [*In a whisper.*] It wasn't you, Darius, that I fought. Try to believe that, try to understand that what I have done I had to do, for I couldn't do otherwise. [*After a pause, overcoming his emotion.*] Don't make a story of this, Hephaestion. Don't say that Alexander, when he saw the dead Darius, begged his forgiveness and wept.

HEPHAESTION. I shall say nothing, Alexander.

ALEXANDER. We shall send him to Persepolis. He shall be buried in the tomb of the Kings, beside his wife. You must go to Babylon, Hephaestion, to break the news to his mother. [HEPHAESTION *nods.*] I never thought it would be like this.

HEPHAESTION. In a farm-cart. Do you remember Gordium?

ALEXANDER. Gordium? The waggon in the citadel? Yes, I remember.

HEPHAESTION. The empire of the world in a farm-cart—and there it is.

ALEXANDER. There it is. I took your mantle once, Darius. Now you can take mine. [ALEXANDER *takes off his white cloak and covers the body with it.*] And after all, Hephaestion, I never did solve that puzzle, did I? How can one solve a puzzle with a sword?

He looks at HEPHAESTION, *who does not reply.*

THE LIGHTS FADE

SCENE TWO

ALEXANDER'S *tent. Its original finery, which had been removed the last time we saw it, has now been largely restored.* PERDICCAS, PTOLEMY *amd* CLEITUS *are standing by the throne.* ALEXANDER, *wearing the robes and crown of Persian royalty, is sitting on the throne. He nods to* MAZARES, *standing on his right, who waves his staff of office to a sentry at the entrance.* BESSUS *a bedraggled but impassive figure, is marched in by two soldiers.* PTOLEMY *reads from a roll.*

PTOLEMY. Alexander, King of Macedon, Captain-General of Greece, Pharaoh of Egypt, King of Babylonia, Lord of the Lands, Great King of Persia and Master of the World, does hereby pronounce that you, Bessus, former Satrap and Prince of Bactria, have been found guilty of all the crimes of which you have been accused before him; to wit, first, that you did make an armed and treacherous rebellion against your rightful sovereign, King Alexander——

BESSUS. Alexander is not my rightful sovereign.

CLEITUS. Silence!

PTOLEMY [*continuing to read*] ——and that you did thereby cause the death of many of His Majesty's loyal subjects; second, that you did for the aim and purpose of making this same armed rebellion, usurp to yourself the false and sacrilegious style of Artaxerxes IV, rightful Great King of Persia; third, that you did commit the crime of most blasphemous murder against the royal and sacred person of his late Imperial Majesty, Darius. For all these crimes he does now sentence you to be taken from here to the city of Ecbatana and there to be put to death in whatever manner the High Council of Medes and Persians, in session there, shall devise. Bessus—former Prince of Bactria—have you anything to say against this sentence?

BESSUS. I have a favour to ask.

PTOLEMY. Ask it.

BESSUS. I am a soldier. All that I have done—even the killing of Darius, to which I freely confessed—has been done in fighting for my country against my country's invader. I am ready now to meet my death. But I would like to meet it as a soldier—not as a felon. Besides—possessing, as I do, a fairly close knowledge of Persian judicial customs—possibly closer than the present Great King of Persia himself——

PTOLEMY. Enough of that——

ALEXANDER *puts his hand on* PTOLEMY'S *arm, restraining him. He nods to* BESSUS *to continue.*

BESSUS. ——it is, therefore, not hard for me to guess the sort of death which the Council of Medes and Persians may devise for a regicide. It will be—to say the least—uncomfortable. I am not afraid of it. I would just rather not meet it. The favour I ask is to be allowed a military execution—here in your camp.

There is a pause. ALEXANDER, *who has barely moved in his throne during all this time, appears to be considering.*

ALEXANDER [*at length*]. The favour is refused.

PTOLEMY *kneels down to the throne, and presents to* ALEXANDER *the document from which he has read.* MAZARES, *kneeling the other side, hands* ALEXANDER *a pen.* ALEXANDER *scribbles his signature.* PTOLEMY *hands it to one of the two soldiers, and signs to him to have* BESSUS *taken out.* BESSUS *faces* ALEXANDER *for a moment, then is turned roughly by the two soldiers and marched out.*

PTOLEMY [*relaxing*]. Well. So much for King Artaxerxes IV—God help him——

ALEXANDER *does not relax his attitude staring thoughtfully in front of him.*

CLEITUS. Alexander——

ALEXANDER. Yes, Cleitus?

CLEITUS. I think you might have granted his request. It wasn't unreasonable.

ALEXANDER. It *was* unreasonable. He killed Darius.

He gets down from the throne and hands his crown to MAZARES, *who goes into the inner apartment.*

CLEITUS. Well?

ALEXANDER. You seem to forget that I'm his lawful successor. He nominated me.

CLEITUS. In a delirium.

ALEXANDER. He knew what he was saying.

CLEITUS. Who believes it, anyway?

ALEXANDER. No one, yet. But the whole world will.

CLEITUS. I don't see why it's so important.

ALEXANDER. Do you want to get home, Cleitus?

CLEITUS. You know I do.

ALEXANDER. Yes. I know you do. I know that all of you do. Now that Darius is dead and Bessus is captured, and we're all of us rich, why can't we go home? That's what you're all asking when I'm not there.

PTOLEMY. Sir——

ALEXANDER. Don't trouble to deny it, Ptolemy. I have ways of finding these things out. I need to have. [*There is an uncomfortable silence.*] Well, here's your answer. We can't go home until we have consolidated what we have gained. And we can't do that until the Persians have ceased to think of us as barbarian conquerors and have come to accept us as their lawful masters. I am the rightful Great King of Persia—in the true line of succession—and so that the world should know that, I have today decreed the punishment of my royal predecessor's murderer—not according to the military law of the Greeks as he requested—but according to the civil law of the Medes and Persians, as is fitting and just for a regicide. Are you answered, Cleitus?

CLEITUS. Yes, sir, I suppose so. It was only that I felt sorry for him.

ALEXANDER. Do you think I didn't?

CLEITUS [*putting an arm round his shoulder*]. I'm sorry. I'm a tactless old fool—as you said.

ALEXANDER. You're Father Cleitus—and I wouldn't have you changed. Now, gentlemen, I take it you've all received your orders for our march into Sogdiana. Are there any comments?

PERDICCAS. The date you have given for the junction of the four columns at Samarkand—isn't it too soon, sir? The country is even wilder and more mountainous than this, I understand, and ideal for guerilla warfare. I don't see how we can clean it up effectively in the time——

ALEXANDER. The date stands. And when I receive your reports in Samarkand I shall expect to hear that all resistance is at an end. By the first days of spring we must be ready to cross the mountains into India——

PTOLEMY. India? So the rumours are true——

ALEXANDER. Yes, Ptolemy. The rumours are true. What comments have you to make?

PTOLEMY [*hastily*]. None, sir, none. Except that I'm told the Indians are rather—numerous——

ALEXANDER. So were the Persians.

PERDICCAS. Does the invasion of India come under the head of consolidation, sir?

ALEXANDER. Yes. Take a look at a map and you'll see why.

CLEITUS [*with a sigh*]. God in heaven! India! We'll never get home—I can see that now. I don't know what my poor wife's going to say.

PTOLEMY. Send her back an elephant to do her shopping on, Cleitus. She'll forgive you, then——

ALEXANDER. In Samarkand I shall have my plan of campaign ready. We can discuss it then. Well, gentlemen, is there anything else?

PTOLEMY. Yes, sir. I've had a report this morning from Herat. Rather serious, I'm afraid. Our garrison there has been wiped out by insurgents led by some local chieftain, called, let me see—Oxyartes. Apparently he——

CLEITUS. Oxyartes? The old rat! It was I who negotiated terms with him——

ALEXANDER. Ptolemy, organise a punitive expedition.

PTOLEMY. Yes, sir.

ALEXANDER. And this time see that you leave a stronger garrison behind.

PTOLEMY. These garrison duties are just about the most unpopular there are in the army just now. Suicide jobs, they're called. Pretty soon, they'll start to desert——

ALEXANDER. Is there no way of pacifying this devil's country? [*To* CLEITUS]. Didn't you take hostages from this man?

CLEITUS. Yes, sir. I took his daughter.

ALEXANDER [*to* PTOLEMY]. Throw him her head as a present. [*To* CLEITUS]. Where is she? In the camp?

CLEITUS [*embarrassed*]. Yes, sir. In fact, sir—I think, of course I may be wrong, but I think you know her——

ALEXANDER. I know her?

CLEITUS. I—er—sent her in to you the other night with one or two other—captives—and—er——

ALEXANDER. Well?

CLEITUS. She was the one who stayed.

ALEXANDER [*calling*]. Roxana! [A GIRL *comes in and stands obediently in the entrance, with eyes lowered.*] Is this the girl you mean?

CLEITUS. Yes, that's the one. Well, well, well.

PTOLEMY [*with a grin*]. I imagine, sir, that now you'll be retracting that order you gave just now?

ALEXANDER. Why should you imagine that?

PTOLEMY. Well, sir—I thought, in the circumstances——

ALEXANDER. Her father is a traitor and her life is forfeit. No circumstances can alter that.

CLEITUS [*a little shocked at* ALEXANDER'S *tone*]. Do you hear that, my girl? I'm sorry—but your father's been a wicked man——

ALEXANDER. She doesn't understand Greek or Persian. She only speaks some weird mountain dialect.

CLEITUS [*looking at her*]. Pretty enough little face—I will say. [*Embarrassed.*] Well, well. This is a sad business.

ALEXANDER. The murder of my garrison was a sad business, too.

CLEITUS. Yes, of course it was. Of course it was. You know, sir—I've been thinking. This killing of hostages doesn't seem to work very well in this part of the country—does it?

ALEXANDER. It must be made to work. What do you suggest, then? That I send this girl back to her father with my blessing?

CLEITUS. No, sir. That'd just be stupid. I only thought you might, perhaps—well, do nothing about her at all—except, well, what you *are* doing about her already. I mean when you look at that face, it does really seem a shocking waste, doesn't it?

They all turn to look at ROXANA, *who smiles at them demurely.*

ALEXANDER. We're wasting time. [*To* CLEITUS.] And you're a soft-hearted old idiot. Remember that we've three thousand miles between us and our base. Clemency is a luxury we were able to afford in Babylon, but not here at the eastern limit of the world. Now, is there anything else?

PTOLEMY. Just a minute, sir. Before we leave the subject of the girl. It seems to me that Cleitus, for once, was talking sense just now——

CLEITUS. That'll be enough from you, young Ptolemy——

PTOLEMY [*ignoring him*]. The situation, we're all agreed, needs a pretty drastic solution. As long as these revolts are sporadic and unconnected, there's no great harm done, but if ever there's a league between four or five of these mountain chiefs, and they get across our lines of communication, we'll none of us see our homes again, much less India. That's a development that could happen at any moment, and we're right to fear it.

CLEITUS. You're misquoting me, Ptolemy. I never said I feared anything——

ALEXANDER. Quiet, Cleitus. [*To* PTOLEMY.] Go on.

PTOLEMY. There are only two alternative policies, terrorism and conciliation.

PERDICCAS. We've tried both, and both have failed.

PTOLEMY. Yes. For one reason only. They've both been half-hearted. If we'd had enough men, terrorism would not have failed. Nor would conciliation, if it had been whole-hearted.

ALEXANDER [*violently*]. In the name of God, Ptolemy! What do you want me to do? I can't make advances to the whole Bactrian race.

PTOLEMY [*smoothly*]. But that's exactly what you can do, sir——

ALEXANDER. What?

PTOLEMY. Through the very attractive person of this Bactrian lady. [*He indicates* ROXANA.] If you want to pacify Bactria in a few days, at no cost whatever, and for good, there, sir, stands your way.

There is a pause. Then CLEITUS *explodes.*

CLEITUS. You're surely not suggesting, Ptolemy, what I think you're suggesting?

PTOLEMY [*defiantly*]. Certainly I am.

CLEITUS. That Alexander should marry this girl?

PTOLEMY. It doesn't have to be a proper marriage—I mean—not according to our rites.

CLEITUS. The King of Macedon and Emperor of the World marrying a barbarian peasant girl?

PTOLEMY. She's not a peasant girl. She's the daughter of an important Bactrian chieftain—a sort of Princess in her own right. [*To* ROXANA.] Aren't you, my girl?

ROXANA, *realising she is being addressed, bows gravely with demure dignity.*

CLEITUS. It's the maddest idea I've ever heard. It would make Alexander the laughing stock of the world.

PTOLEMY. I don't think somehow—whatever Alexander did—he could be quite that. Besides we can make up a fine story about it. The captive maid. Love at first sight. The chivalrous conqueror insisting on marriage—all that——

PERDICCAS. Really, Ptolemy. I didn't know you had so much imagination.

PTOLEMY [*stubbornly*]. Well—if you want to impress the local chiefs it seems to me a far better way of doing it than by chucking her father her head. And we've just got to impress them if we want to live, and I for one am not ashamed to admit that I do.

He turns and looks at ALEXANDER, *as do the others.* ALEXANDER *laughs.*

ALEXANDER. I'm glad you've all remembered that the prospective bridegroom might be expected to have some say in the matter.

PTOLEMY. Of course, sir—it's for you to decide.

ALEXANDER. Thank you, Ptolemy. I shall. Leave me now, will you. I have Philotas being brought in in a moment.

PERDICCAS. Oh. Shouldn't we stay for that?

ALEXANDER. No. I must see him alone.

PERDICCAS. Better have the sentries in.

ALEXANDER. You insult me, Perdiccas. Do you think I'm afraid of an unarmed man?

PERDICCAS. A desperate man.

ALEXANDER. So am I a desperate man.

PERDICCAS. Yes, sir.

He goes out.

PTOLEMY. Think over my suggestion, won't you?

ALEXANDER. I appreciate your match-making efforts.

PTOLEMY. It's not such a mad idea as it sounds, you know.

ALEXANDER. I know.

CLEITUS. Of course it's mad. But it's worse than mad. It's obscene. If you have any regard for me at all, I beg you not to listen to it.

ALEXANDER. I have regard for you, Father Cleitus. Great regard. But not more than I have for the lives of my men. And so I must listen. [*To* PTOLEMY.] It would be a terrible risk.

PTOLEMY. Alexander—frightened of a risk?

ALEXANDER. Of this one, he is. I think I'll decide no.

CLEITUS [*delighted*]. Good boy! I mean, Your Majesty has made a wise decision.

He goes out.

PTOLEMY. Think it over, sir.

He goes out. ALEXANDER *turns and looks at* ROXANA. *She raises her eyes to him. He takes her chin in his hand.*

ALEXANDER. Love at first sight? The chivalrous conqueror? Or—— [*He pulls the side of his hand across her throat. She smiles.*] At least you'd have one valuable asset as a wife. You can't talk. [*Gently.*] Go away.

He nods towards the inner apartment. She nods, bows and walks gracefully out. ALEXANDER *goes back to the table and looks through some documents. He pours himself a cup of wine and drains it in a gulp, refilling the cup at once.* HEPHAESTION *comes in.*

HEPHAESTION. Alexander.

ALEXANDER [*delightedly*]. Hephaestion! [*He jumps up and embraces him.*] Thank God you're back. When did you arrive?

HEPHAESTION. An hour ago.

ALEXANDER. You look well. Was it a troublesome journey?

HEPHAESTION. It was a long one. You've covered a good deal of ground since I saw you last.

ALEXANDER. I shall have covered a lot more in a few months. Tomorrow we march on Samarkand—across the River of the Sands. Then on to the last river—the great River of the Sea. There I intend to found another city. I shall call it Alexandria-at-the-end-of-the-World. How do you like the name?

HEPHAESTION. It sounds a little sad.

ALEXANDER. Does it? To me it sounds magnificent. Have some wine?

HEPHAESTION. Thank you.

ALEXANDER *pours out a cup and replenishes his own.*

ALEXANDER [*toasting*]. To another world beyond this one.

HEPHAESTION [*smiling*]. A world of ghosts?

ALEXANDER. No. A world of men. You can't fight ghosts.

HEPHAESTION. You can't conquer them.

A SOLDIER *enters and salutes.*

ALEXANDER. Bring him in. [*He turns to face the opening as* PHILOTAS *is brought in. He looks ill and broken, and limps heavily. His hands are chained.*] [*Sharply.*] Why has he been chained?

SOLDIER. General Ptolemy's orders, sir—a week ago.

ALEXANDER [*angrily*]. How dare he give such an order? Philotas, will you believe me when I say I had nothing to do with this?

PHILOTAS [*lightly*]. Yes, Alexander, I'll believe you. Hullo, Hephaestion. How are you? You might have come to see me in prison. Alexander did often. He wept over me once. I was most touched. Of course he hasn't been for the last week to see me wearing my new decorations.

He extends his manacled hands.

HEPHAESTION. I couldn't have come. I've been in Babylon.

PHILOTAS. In Babylon? Did you see my father?

HEPHAESTION. Yes. He sent you many messages.

PHILOTAS. He doesn't know?

HEPHAESTION. No.

PHILOTAS. Good. How is he?

HEPHAESTION. Very well.

ALEXANDER [*to the* SOLDIER]. Have these things taken off his hands.

SOLDIER. Yes, sir.

PHILOTAS *goes out, followed by the soldier. There is an uneasy pause after he has gone.*

HEPHAESTION. It's true then?

ALEXANDER. Didn't you get my despatch?

HEPHAESTION. Yes, but I thought perhaps—you told me so little, Alexander—I found it hard to believe——

ALEXANDER. I had no doubt you would. [*A shade scornfully.*] Well—what was it you thought perhaps?

HEPHAESTION. That you'd only had him arrested for a day or two, to teach him a sharp lesson—that he would be free again now.

ALEXANDER. Philotas was arrested two months ago. His trial is next week.

HEPHAESTION [*miserably*]. He's guilty, then?

ALEXANDER. Of what?

HEPHAESTION. Of plotting against your life.

ALEXANDER. No. He's innocent of that.

HEPHAESTION. Thank God!

ALEXANDER. There *was* a plot against my life. A lunatic called Dymnos conceived an idea I'd be better dead. Like most of my men, he wanted to get home to his wife and no doubt thought that was the quickest way back to Macedon. Of course he chattered about his idea to someone, who told someone else, who told someone else, who reported it to Philotas. Philotas did nothing. He claims he thought the story an hysterical invention. But meanwhile my own agents had heard of the rumour and arrested this Dymnos, who promptly cut his throat with the dagger he had been sharpening for me. The whole affair would have been supremely unimportant if it hadn't been for Philotas' part in it. At the time his negligence looked a little suspicious—to say the least——

HEPHAESTION. But now you know him to be innocent?

ALEXANDER. Yes. I know him now to be innocent—of that charge.

HEPHAESTION. There are others, then?

ALEXANDER. Many.

HEPHAESTION. Are they serious?

ALEXANDER. So the High Council of the Army believes.

HEPHAESTION. What do you believe?

ALEXANDER. What I believe isn't important.

HEPHAESTION. But of course it is——

ALEXANDER. I shan't be here for the trial. [HEPHAESTION *stares at him.* ALEXANDER *fills another cup of wine, offering it to* HEPHAESTION, *who shakes his head.*] You saw Parmenion in Babylon?

HEPHAESTION. Yes.

ALEXANDER. You told him nothing about his son?

HEPHAESTION. Of course not. [*Pause.*]

ALEXANDER. And the Queen-Mother is still firm in her resolve to punish me for the death of Darius?

HEPHAESTION. She says I'm to tell you that her feelings for you have not changed.

ALEXANDER. But will never see me, or speak to me, or write to me again? [HEPHAESTION *nods.*] Has she forgotten that I can command her to do all these things?

HEPHAESTION. No. She is the mother of Darius.

ALEXANDER [*slowly*]. Perhaps I'd better teach her who *I* am. [PHILOTAS *enters.*] [*Putting a stool for him.*] Sit down, Philotas.

PHILOTAS. It might be as well. Some of your interrogations have lately been a little—severe.

He sits on the stool.

ALEXANDER. They are not *my* interrogations. You're in the hands of the High Council of the Army. I have nothing to do with it.

PHILOTAS. Haven't you?

ALEXANDER [*to* PHILOTAS]. A cup of wine?

PHILOTAS. Of course. Have you ever known me to refuse? [ALEXANDER *hands him a cup.*] Thank you. [*He takes a sip.*] I've been trying lately to remember what wine tasted like. I notice that the reality is better than my imagination made it. I've no doubt the same is true of other pleasures. How is Antigone, by the way?

ALEXANDER. Well, I believe.

PHILOTAS. I think you might have allowed her to see me——

ALEXANDER. The Council refused permission. She's a witness against you.

PHILOTAS *meditatively takes another sip of wine.*

PHILOTAS. I loved that bitch.

ALEXANDER. The case against you, I'm afraid, is very strong.

PHILOTAS. I've no doubt of that. No doubt at all.

ALEXANDER. I know you don't believe it, Philotas—but I want to help you.

PHILOTAS. Help me, then. Set me free. Give me back my command and punish my accusers.

ALEXANDER [*picking up a document*]. You are your own chief accuser. Shall I read you some of the things you are reported to have said?

PHILOTAS. What a man says in bed should never be held against him.

ALEXANDER. Those things weren't only said in bed. Nor only to Antigone. Shall I read some of them?

PHILOTAS. If you must. Let me have another cup of wine meanwhile. I'd better make the best of these few minutes.

HEPHAESTION *fills his cup.*

ALEXANDER [*reading*]. The greatness of a man is to be measured not by what he does but by what he is. On that premise Alexander is about as great as my little finger.

PHILOTAS. Yes. I remember when I said that. It was at a banquet in Egypt. I was drunk.

ALEXANDER. Not too drunk to remember having said it. [*Reading.*] People say Alexander is a god. Surely the place for a god is on Olympus—not on the throne of Asia.

PHILOTAS. An unexceptionable sentiment, I should have thought, from an atheist.

ALEXANDER. The Council may not find it so.

PHILOTAS. Is it a crime to make a joke?

ALEXANDER. Was it a joke?

PHILOTAS. As much of a joke as people saying you're a god.

ALEXANDER *looks at him for a moment, then returns to the document.*

ALEXANDER [*reading*]. We began as the Companions of a Macedonian adventurer. We've ended as the slaves of an oriental despot. [*He looks up.*] Was that, too, a joke?

PHILOTAS. No. I think that was true.

ALEXANDER. You see, Hephaestion, what can I do? He is bent

on self-murder. [*To* PHILOTAS.] Philotas—it is you who are making an oriental despot of me. [*Sincerely*.] How can you think that that is what I want to be? I shudder at the very thought. Can't you forget for a moment who and what I am now, and think of me as the simple Greek soldier who once was your friend?

PHILOTAS. Yes, Alexander, I can. A little too easily, perhaps, for my peace of mind.

ALEXANDER. For all that, Philotas, I am *still* your friend, and determined, if I can, to save you from yourself. You call me a despot. What else can I be? How can this vast empire be ruled but by despotism? Like Athens—with a democratic revolution every year? You say I make myself a god. Do you remember Aristotle—my tutor in the old days? You remember what he used to say to us all? The true King is a god among men—bound no more than Zeus by country or law—because he himself is the law? Can you blame me then, if, in the loneliness of my present state I sometimes think of myself as the kin of God? It's a small comfort and seems to me to harm no one——

PHILOTAS. No one but yourself.

ALEXANDER [*savagely*]. What is that to you? I give you the lie, Philotas. What a man *is*—is nothing. What a man does is everything. I don't know—and don't care—what I *am*—or what I do to myself with my thoughts and deeds. I do know—and do care—what I've *done*; and what I've done I shall not allow to be destroyed either by the actions of my enemies or the taunts and jeers of my friends. Which is why, in a few days' time, you—my dear friend—may have to die; for this document will be your death warrant, if I give it to the Council.

PHILOTAS. Then why give it them?

ALEXANDER. I shall burn it, if you fulfil one small condition——

PHILOTAS. That I fall down in public and worship you as a god?

ALEXANDER. That you make a speech at your trial in which you retract every word you've ever said against me; and that you swear to me, now, on the most solemn oath you know, that you will never say another as long as you live.

PHILOTAS *looks at* ALEXANDER *for a moment.*

PHILOTAS [*quietly*]. But that's what I just said, Alexander. That I fall down in public and worship you as a god. [*He gets up and puts the cup on the table.*] Thank you for the wine, Alexander. [*Calling.*] Guard. [*The* SOLDIER *comes in.*] Take the assassin back to his gaol.

ALEXANDER [*taking him by the arm*]. Philotas—I beg of you—think before you do this——

PHILOTAS. Oh, I've thought, Alexander. I've thought quite long enough. What else do you suppose I do in my cell all day—and all night? I'm tired of thinking.

ALEXANDER. What I ask of you is not a great thing to ask of a friend.

PHILOTAS. It's a small thing to ask of an enemy. If you were Darius, I would be a fool not to save my life on such terms. But you're not—you're Alexander—and what you ask is greater than the world we've conquered together.

ALEXANDER. Do you expect me to have mercy for you?

PHILOTAS. No. I understand what you must do.

ALEXANDER. Philotas. Have pity on me—if not on yourself.

PHILOTAS. I have, strange to say. Pity on both of us. [*He brushes his eyes with his hand.*] I shouldn't have had that second drink. It was a mistake on an empty stomach. Goodbye. [*He holds out his hand.* ALEXANDER *grasps it.*] I've enjoyed the adventure. I wish I could have seen how it ended. Goodbye, Hephaestion.

HEPHAESTION. Philotas—I beg you—do what Alexander asks—

PHILOTAS. I'm not Alexander—that's the trouble. I can't do the impossible. [*To the* SOLDIER.] Come on, my friend. Forward march. [*Turning at the entrance.*] I didn't try to kill you, you know; but if you should be fool enough to pardon me now, I would. And I wouldn't bungle it, either, like that fool Dymnos.

He goes out, followed by the SOLDIER. ALEXANDER, *plainly affected, looks at* HEPHAESTION, *who stares at him saying nothing.* ALEXANDER *pours himself another cup of wine.*

ALEXANDER [*at length*]. Hephaestion—I am giving you an order.

HEPHAESTION. Yes, Alexander?

ALEXANDER. There is no one else I can ask it of.

HEPHAESTION. I am glad of that.

ALEXANDER. You must return to Babylon at once, take a battalion of foot guards, and put Parmenion under arrest.

HEPHAESTION [*uncomprehending*]. Parmenion?

ALEXANDER. Yes. Parmenion.

HEPHAESTION. But why? What has he done?

ALEXANDER. Nothing, yet.

HEPHAESTION. Then on what charge am I to arrest him?

ALEXANDER. Protective custody. The men's anger will be so great when they hear of Philotas' treachery that they may turn on Philotas' father.

HEPHAESTION. But you don't believe that, do you? Parmenion is worshipped by his men.

ALEXANDER [*harshly*]. It's not good for a mortal to be worshipped. Didn't you hear Philotas say that? And Parmenion has far too many men to worship him.

HEPHAESTION. You're afraid of him?

ALEXANDER. With some reason. He controls the heart of my empire. Damn all the Gods! Why did I leave him there? I must have been mad.

HEPHAESTION. Alexander—I'd stake my life on Parmenion's loyalty.

ALEXANDER. You'd better not. Your life is too precious to me.

HEPHAESTION. What makes you think——

ALEXANDER. God—but you enrage me, sometimes, Hephaestion.

HEPHAESTION. I'm sorry.

ALEXANDER. You see everything as it is. Nothing, ever, as it might be. Parmenion is loyal, you say, because he always has been. I agree—or I would hardly have left him in Babylon at the head of an independent army. But then, when I did that I didn't guess that I was going to execute his son.

HEPHAESTION. I'm not trying to shirk the duty. Let me go to him alone, unarmed, without escort, and break the news——

ALEXANDER. And present a prospective rebel with the most valuable hostage I have to give?

HEPHAESTION. I don't believe that he is a prospective rebel.

ALEXANDER. I don't intend to wait to find that out. These are your instructions, Hephaestion. You will go to Babylon and stay at the Palace, disposing your men there unobtrusively under arms to reinforce the Persian guard. You will send a message to Parmenion at his headquarters requiring his presence at the Palace. You'd better say you have an important despatch from me, and that you are ill and can't go to him yourself. Philotas' trial is not for another week. There is no reason why Parmenion should be suspicious.

HEPHAESTION. No reason.

ALEXANDER. Afterwards you must read a proclamation to the troops. I shall write it for you, and it will have my signature and seal on it. I shall declare that I have incontrovertible proof that Parmenion—like his son—had been plotting against me.

HEPHAESTION [*with a start*]. *Had* been?

ALEXANDER. He must die resisting arrest.

HEPHAESTION. No.

ALEXANDER. There's no other way.

HEPHAESTION. No, Alexander——

ALEXANDER. Do you think I like to give you that order? How can I risk an open trial, when I have no evidence? How can I leave him guarded by one battalion, in a town where fifteen thousand of his own men are under arms? He must be killed on the spot. It's the only possible thing to do.

HEPHAESTION. Then you must find someone else to do it. Not myself.

ALEXANDER. It must be you. You're the only one I can trust.

HEPHAESTION. You're wrong, Alexander. In this you can't trust me. If I went to Babylon I would betray you.

ALEXANDER. I'll take that risk.

HEPHAESTION. *I* won't. You must find someone else.

ALEXANDER. You'll disobey an order?

HEPHAESTION. This order. You can order me now to fall on my sword. That I should obey. Even for you I won't commit murder.

ALEXANDER. Have I such a weakling for a friend?

HEPHAESTION [*miserably*]. Yes. Why don't you have me killed too?

ALEXANDER. I must let the Gods do that. Surely they must envy such dazzling virtue, such nobility of character in a mere mortal. It's a wonder they've let you live so long—Hephaestion.

HEPHAESTION. Let me go now——

ALEXANDER. I know now what vows of friendship are worth. I must remember this moment. This is the moment that Alexander first discovered that he had no friend in all the world, and that from now on he must stand alone. Leave me now. And for all I care you need never come back again. [*He stands aside to let* HEPHAESTION *pass him to the entrance.*] Send in Perdiccas.

HEPHAESTION *goes.*

ALEXANDER [*calling*]. Mazares. [MAZARES *appears.* ALEXANDER *sits at the table. His hands are shaking with nervous strain. He looks at them fixedly.*] Do you remember the night before Gaugemela, Mazares?

MAZARES. Yes, Majesty?

ALEXANDER. That night you saw my hands shaking with fear. Do you remember it?

MAZARES. Well, Majesty.

ALEXANDER. My hands are shaking now, Mazares, and yet I have no battle to fight tomorrow. [*Laughing a little drunkenly.*] If only I had. [ALEXANDER *hands him a beaker.* MAZARES *takes it, bows low.*] Fill this. [MAZARES *backs out.* ALEXANDER *begins to write.* ROXANA *comes in, with a beaker of wine. She quietly takes* ALEXANDER'S *cup and fills it for him. He takes it automatically, thinking it is* MAZARES, *then looks up and sees her.*] I'd forgotten you'd appointed yourself my cup-bearer, Roxana. Thank you. [*She smiles at him and sits on the stool at his side.*] What toast shall I give you? A loyal toast? Death to all the King's enemies? I think that'll do very well. Here's death to all the King's enemies! [*He drinks.* ROXANA *lays her hand timidly on his arm. He kisses it.*] That includes, of course, your father, which is rather a pity. But then we can't help that can we? Do you love your father, Roxana? Does he love you? [ROXANA *laughs at him gaily.*] You find the very idea ridiculous. I see, and who am I to blame you? Here. [*He hands her his cup and she takes a sip.*] Drink to his perdition in a loving cup. That's right. Now you must leave me. I have other enemies to deal with beside your father. The Master of the World has many enemies, you know, Roxana. He doesn't want to have enemies. He wants everyone to love him. But he also wants to remain Master of the World. [*Pushing her gently.*] Now go. [*She moves to the door.* ALEXANDER *suddenly slips off a ring from his finger.*] Roxana. [*He signals her to stop, then pull out a small dagger from his belt. He approaches her and stretches out his hands.*] You see, Roxana—in one hand, a ring—a very pretty ring. It belonged to my mother. In the other hand a dagger—also a very pretty one. That belonged to my father. Now let's play a little game. You must choose which hand—the right or the left. [*He touches her two arms to show her what he means. She smiles delightedly. Then he puts his hands behind him and juggles the two objects. Still keeping them behind him he nods to her to choose. After a little thought she touches his left arm. He brings that hand out and shows her the ring. He throws the dagger point downwards on to the table, and slips the ring on to her finger.*

ALEXANDER. Yes. I think you'll make a good wife, Roxana. You also, I see, have the quality of luck.

He kisses her, then turns brusquely from her and goes back to the table. He begins to write. ROXANA *curtsies very low and goes out, delightedly admiring her ring.*

THE LIGHTS FADE

SCENE THREE

The gardens at Babylon. The QUEEN-MOTHER *is reading a document, sitting at her usual place on the bench.* PERDICCAS *is standing near her, watching her. The* QUEEN-MOTHER *lowers the document, and stares thoughtfully at the horizon.*

PERDICCAS. Perhaps that explains the matter better than I can.

QUEEN-MOTHER. It explains it perfectly. I am your prisoner.

PERDICCAS. Oh no, ma'am. The King has simply expressed a wish to see you before he leaves for India——

QUEEN-MOTHER. When a King expresses a wish in such terms it is usually better described as a command. And when he sends one of his most trusted generals and a battalion of guards to carry it out——

PERDICCAS. Escorting you to the King is not my only duty in Babylon, ma'am. I have another.

QUEEN-MOTHER. What? Oh! I suppose I mustn't ask. Very well—General. When do we leave?

PERDICCAS. Tomorrow.

QUEEN-MOTHER. I see. And where is the King now?

PERDICCAS. At the moment Samarkand; but, by the time we reach him he expects to be two or three hundred miles further east.

QUEEN-MOTHER. He must be careful he doesn't fall over the edge of the world.

PERDICCAS. He believes he'll reach it soon.

QUEEN-MOTHER. I expect he will. [*Smiling at* PERDICCAS.] Well General, if, at my time of life, I have to travel to the end of the world, I am delighted that it should be in such charming company.

PERDICCAS. Your journey will be as comfortable as I can make it.

QUEEN-MOTHER. Thank you, sir. It would have been kinder of Alexander to have sent Philotas on this mission. His father is very lonely here in Babylon, and I know would have given much for a sight of him.

PERDICCAS. Philotas is under arrest.

QUEEN-MOTHER. Under arrest? What is the charge?

PERDICCAS. High treason.

QUEEN-MOTHER. I see. Poor Alexander.

PERDICCAS. Ma'am?

QUEEN-MOTHER. I said, poor Alexander.

PERDICCAS. I don't understand you, ma'am.

QUEEN-MOTHER. I hardly thought you would, General. I won't detain you any longer. I know you have other duties to perform.

PERDICCAS. I have.

QUEEN-MOTHER. I shall be ready for you at dawn.

She bows to him, dismissing him. He bows back and goes out R. The QUEEN-MOTHER *looks at the document in her hand again. There is the sound of the* PRINCESS' *voice off, laughing gaily. She comes on in a moment, L., accompanied by* PARMENION.

PRINCESS. Grandmother—look who I found walking in the gardens——

QUEEN-MOTHER. General Parmenion—how good of you to come and see us——

PARMENION. I am afraid it isn't pleasure that's brought me to the Palace, today, ma'am. It's duty. I have to see Perdiccas.

QUEEN-MOTHER. Oh yes? You'll find him in the Palace.

PARMENION. I understood he was ill in bed.

QUEEN-MOTHER. Well, he's not in bed. I can vouch for that. He left me here a minute ago. As for being ill he may be—but he was concealing it very well.

PARMENION. Strange. I had a message saying he was in bed——

PRINCESS [*looking over* QUEEN-MOTHER'S *shoulder*.] Oh, grandmother—that's Alexander's writing. Let me see——

QUEEN-MOTHER. No, dear. He sends you his love.

PRINCESS. What else does he say?

QUEEN-MOTHER. He wants me to go and see him. Darling, I'm afraid I shall have to leave you here alone for a few months—will you mind?

PRINCESS. Oh, grandmother—can't I come too?

QUEEN-MOTHER. No, darling.

PRINCESS. Oh, grandmother! But why are *you* going, then? You swore you'd never speak to him again.

QUEEN-MOTHER. I've changed my mind.

PARMENION. You must act as my courier to Alexander, ma'am. I'll give you many messages for him.

QUEEN-MOTHER. I shall be glad to take them.

PARMENION. And, of course, to my son.

QUEEN-MOTHER. Yes, of course.

PARMENION. There's a rumour the young scamp's in trouble. Been cheeking Alexander again, I expect. I gather they've given his command to Cleitus.

QUEEN-MOTHER [*murmuring*]. I'm sorry.

PARMENION. Oh, it won't do him any harm. Teach him a useful lesson, I hope. Can't say I like the idea of an infantryman in charge of cavalry, though. Still, I suppose Alexander knows what he's doing——

PRINCESS [*looking off*]. Look—grandmother—there are some more soldiers over there.

QUEEN-MOTHER. Yes, there are.

PRINCESS. There are an awful lot of them. And there are twice as many Persian guards as usual. Why's that, grandmother?

QUEEN-MOTHER. I expect they're guarding General Perdiccas.

PARMENION. Perdiccas!

PRINCESS. Oh. Is he very important?

QUEEN-MOTHER. Very important.

PARMENION. Perdiccas important? First I've heard of it.

PRINCESS. I think there's something up. Something exciting.

PARMENION. I must leave you——

The QUEEN-MOTHER *gets up abruptly. She is looking, suddenly. tense and worried.*

QUEEN-MOTHER. General Parmenion?

PARMENION [*stopping*]. Yes, ma'am?

QUEEN-MOTHER. Which gate did you use?

PARMENION. Your own, ma'am. I took the liberty of coming through your private apartments. I hope you don't mind—but you did say——

QUEEN-MOTHER. Did anyone see you?

PARMENION. No.

QUEEN-MOTHER. No one was guarding the gate?

PARMENION. No. There never is.

QUEEN-MOTHER. Will you think me very foolish and hysterical if I ask you to do something? Will you go back at once to your own headquarters—using the same gate—and send down a message to Perdiccas saying that *you* are ill and that if he wants to see you he must come to you?

PARMENION. But I'm not ill.

QUEEN-MOTHER [*significantly*]. Neither is Perdiccas.

He looks at her and suddenly gets her meaning.

PARMENION. No . . . no more he is. [*He looks off in the direction in which the* PRINCESS *has pointed at the* SOLDIERS.] Alexander's own footguards. How many are there in the Palace?

QUEEN-MOTHER. I heard someone say a full battalion.

PARMENION. I see.

QUEEN-MOTHER. Please, General, please. Do what I ask.

PRINCESS. Grandmother—is there anything wrong?

QUEEN-MOTHER. No, dear. [*To* PARMENION.] General—I know you understand me——

[*Pause.*]

PARMENION [*musingly*]. Why, I wonder? It's that that I can't quite understand. Why?

QUEEN-MOTHER. Perdiccas may be——

PARMENION. Perdiccas is nothing. A slow-witted, but highly efficient, field officer. I'd trust him anywhere. Besides, he's here under direct orders from Alexander. I've seen the commission——

QUEEN-MOTHER. Yes. So have I.

PARMENION *strokes his chin, staring at the ground.*

PARMENION [*at length*]. Why, in heaven's name? Can you see that, ma'am? Why?

QUEEN-MOTHER. I think that's a question, General, it would serve no purpose to ask.

PARMENION. But I must ask it, ma'am. I must.

QUEEN-MOTHER. Perhaps—you said yourself that your son——

PARMENION. My son?

QUEEN-MOTHER. I happen to know that his trouble is rather worse than you think it is. [PARMENION *sits down suddenly.*] General—this may be all my imagination——

PARMENION. No, it isn't. I know it now. When one is very old one has this gift for seeing everything in a sudden flash—very clearly—as if it were a pattern on a carpet. Is my son dead?

QUEEN-MOTHER. No, General. I don't think so.

PARMENION. I believe he is.

QUEEN-MOTHER [*comfortingly*]. Try not to think of him, at the moment. Think of yourself.

PARMENION. Yes. I must do that, mustn't I? [*He gets up quickly.*] When you see Alexander give him this from me, will you? [*He takes a locket off his neck.*] It was given me by his father. He might like to have it back. Goodbye, ma'am, and thank you for being a very true friend. [*He kisses her hand. To* PRINCESS.] Goodbye, my little lady. Take care of yourself.

PRINCESS. Goodbye.

QUEEN-MOTHER [*pointing*]. When you leave the Palace keep close to the trees and they won't see you—— [*He unbuckles his sword and lays it on the ground. Then he moves in the opposite direction from that in which the* QUEEN-MOTHER *is pointing.*] [*Startled.*] General—you're not going to——

PARMENION [*turning*]. I'm going to see Perdiccas. He has a message for me from Alexander. So, of course, I shan't need my sword. Goodbye.

He bows to the QUEEN-MOTHER, *who is staring at him in alarm, and goes off the opposite way from which he has come. The* QUEEN-MOTHER *and the* PRINCESS *look after him in silence.*

THE LIGHTS FADE

SCENE FOUR

ALEXANDER'S *tent. The divans which first decorated the tent have now replaced the bare table and stools, and on one of them* ALEXANDER *is lying, a cup of wine in his hand.* PTOLEMY *is lying on another.* CLEITUS *is standing. Both are also drinking.*

ALEXANDER. There are five main rivers in India and beyond the fifth lies the southern end of the world.

PTOLEMY. I look forward to seeing that.

CLEITUS. I don't. There's only one place I look forward to seeing and I think you both know where that is.

PTOLEMY [*with a laugh*]. Pella. That's an end of the world in a different sense. Personally I don't mind if I never see that primitive little village again——

CLEITUS [*outraged*]. Sir—are you going to lie there and let him insult the capital of your Kingdom?

ALEXANDER. Macedon isn't my Kingdom. It's a province in my Kingdom—and a very small and unimportant province at that.

CLEITUS. Sir!

ALEXANDER. Sit down, Father Cleitus, and have some more wine.

CLEITUS. No, thank you, sir. [*Beginning to withdraw.*] As a matter of fact, sir—I think—if you'll forgive me——

ALEXANDER. Don't be an old fool. Sit down.

CLEITUS. I don't care for jokes against my country.

ALEXANDER *jumps up and puts his arm on his shoulder.*

ALEXANDER. Well—forgive my tactlessness then. Surely you must allow a bridegroom a little latitude on his wedding day. Put it down to pre-nuptial nerves. You can't desert me now, Father, in my hour of need, you who have been at my side in every battle.

CLEITUS. This is one battle in which I'd just as soon not be at your side.

He allows himself to be led back to the table and given another cup of wine.

HEPHAESTION *comes in and stands to attention inside the door.*

HEPHAESTION. You asked to see me, sir.

ALEXANDER. Yes. [*To the others.*] Leave me with Hephaestion a moment. Go in there [*pointing to the inner quarters*] and indulge in the old Persian custom of kissing the bride. Only not too much. And take this. [*He hands them a beaker of wine.*] [PTOLEMY *and* CLEITUS *go out. There is a pause after they have gone, while* ALEXANDER *studies* HEPHAESTION.] About the ceremony. You've read what your part in it is to be?

HEPHAESTION. Yes, sir.

ALEXANDER. There's a banquet afterwards. I shall expect you to be present.

HEPHAESTION. Very well, sir. [*He turns to go.*]

ALEXANDER. And Hephaestion.

HEPHAESTION. Yes, sir?

ALEXANDER. I shall expect you to sit at my right hand.

HEPHAESTION. I see. Thank you. Is that all?

ALEXANDER. No. I see I must humble myself. Will you forgive me, Hephaestion?

HEPHAESTION. There's nothing to forgive, sir.

ALEXANDER [*savagely*]. For the love of God! What do you want me to do? Rend my clothes and pour dust on my head and roll on the ground at your feet? I will if you like. The truth is, Hephaestion, I'm not as invincible as I believed. You've won. I admit defeat, and would like to salute my conqueror. [*He holds out his hand. After a slight pause,* HEPHAESTION *grasps it.*] Sit here. [*He leads him to the divan.*] Parmenion is dead. I had word this morning.

HEPHAESTION. Perdiccas is back?

ALEXANDER. No. He arrives in a week. He sent a courier on ahead. Philotas was executed a month ago.

HEPHAESTION. Yes. I had heard that.

ALEXANDER. I know what you're feeling about me at this moment.

HEPHAESTION. Not about you, Alexander. For you, that's all.

ALEXANDER. Thank you. I've needed you, you know, these last few weeks.

HEPHAESTION. I'm sorry.

ALEXANDER. Cleitus and Ptolemy can't help much with this kind of burden. I'm not a murderer. Will you believe that?

HEPHAESTION. Yes.

ALEXANDER. Despot I am, because I must be. But I still have that ideal—the ideal that began this adventure. The world state. The world state ruled over by the man-god, whose word is law, and who has dedicated his whole life and being to the welfare of all his many million subjects. No more war. No more oppression. No more brigandage. A universal peace, blessed by the Almighty Gods. [*He stops and glances at* HEPHAESTION.] It's not an unworthy vision, is it?

HEPHAESTION. No, Alexander. It isn't.

ALEXANDER. It's now or never, Hephaestion. This is a world grown old and cynical. If I fail, who else shall succeed?

HEPHAESTION. No one.

ALEXANDER. And so I musn't fail. How easy to have pardoned Philotas—to have taken the risk over Parmenion—to have gained for myself the title of Alexander the Kind, Alexander the Merciful—other words for Alexander the Weak, Alexander the Defeated. And Alexander mustn't be defeated —or he will betray both himself and his vision. Have some wine.

HEPHAESTION. No, thank you.

ALEXANDER. Oh come. If never before, you must get drunk on my wedding night. You must forgive me my lecture in political science. Did I sound like Aristotle?

HEPHAESTION [*smiling*]. A little——

CLEITUS *comes in. He is a little drunk.*

CLEITUS. The bride is ready. She wants to show herself to her loving spouse-to-be. May she come out?

ALEXANDER. Yes. Let us inspect Her Majesty.

CLEITUS. [*sharply*]. Her Majesty? She's not going to be that, is she?

ALEXANDER. Just for today—at the ceremony.

CLEITUS. Oh, I see. I was going to say. I mean—a Persian—that would never do. [*Speaking into the inner room.*] All right, my girl. You can come out now.

ROXANA *enters, beautifully and royally dressed.* PTOLEMY *comes in behind her.* ALEXANDER *approaches her.*

ALEXANDER. Your loving husband salutes you. I admire your face and figure almost as much as I do your dowry.

CLEITUS [*pouring himself wine*]. Her dowry?

ALEXANDER. Roughly thirty thousand lives and six months' campaigning. I call that valuable enough, don't you?

CLEITUS. I certainly do. If you've brought me six months nearer home I salute you too, my dear. [*He kisses her on the forehead.*]

ALEXANDER. I must have some more wine. [*He drains his cup and refills it.*] It's a very complicated ceremony, you know. I haven't learnt my part as I should. I only wish the Queen-Mother were here to help me. I should have postponed the ceremony for a week. Dear mother. I long to see her again.

CLEITUS *and* PTOLEMY, *during this, have been talking together and drinking.* CLEITUS *turns at this remark.*

CLEITUS. Why do you call her your mother, Alexander? Your mother is a Macedonian.

ALEXANDER. The Queen-Mother of Persia *is* my mother, Cleitus—just as she is your queen——

CLEITUS. My queen? Olympias of Macedon is my queen—not a wretched Persian——

ALEXANDER [*angrily*]. Cleitus!

PTOLEMY [*alarmed*]. Cleitus—come here.

He takes him by the arm, but CLEITUS *shoves him off.*

CLEITUS. I don't mean any disrespect to you, sir—you know that—but all this bowing and scraping and kneeling to barbarians—it makes me sick——

ALEXANDER [*to* PTOLEMY]. What's the matter with the old man, this evening—apart from wine?

PTOLEMY. I've just told him about your intention to form a corps of Persian Companions for the Indian expedition.

ALEXANDER. Oh. That's what's upset him, is it?

CLEITUS. Persian Companions! What did we fight this war for anyway—that's what I'd like to know. Persian Companions! I suppose they'll be given Macedonian slaves to curl their hair——

PTOLEMY. Cleitus—look——

PTOLEMY *offers* CLEITUS *a drink.*

CLEITUS [*muttering*]. I suppose we'll have Indian Companions next——

ALEXANDER [*pointing to Roxana*]. Do you approve my choice of bride, Hephaestion?

HEPHAESTION. Most emphatically.

ALEXANDER. You're carrying her crown in the procession this evening, aren't you?

HEPHAESTION. No. It's yours I'm carrying——

ALEXANDER. Oh yes. Of course. Who's carrying hers? Cleitus, is it you?

CLEITUS [*coming forward*]. What's that?

ALEXANDER. Are you carrying Roxana's crown in the procession?

CLEITUS. Yes, that's right. I've got it all pat. I walk ahead of her all the way holding the cushion up in the air—my arms'll be near dropping off after a minute or two—and then when we reach the platform I step aside, and let her climb the stairs and sit down and then I go up and put the crown on her head. Correct, sir?

ALEXANDER. Correct, save for one thing. You've forgotten the obeisance.

CLEITUS. Obeisance? What's that?

ALEXANDER. You're to kneel down at the foot of the throne, and place your head to the ground. Heavens, man, you've seen it done often enough.

CLEITUS. Yes. I've seen it done often enough—but I'm not going to do it.

ALEXANDER. You must.

CLEITUS. What, to a Persian? Not on your life.

ALEXANDER. Don't be a fool, Cleitus——

CLEITUS. Fool I may be, but I'm not chewing any dirt in front of any little barbarian——

ALEXANDER. Cleitus—have a care——

PTOLEMY. You volunteered for the duty.

CLEITUS. Yes, I did, but if I'd known there was going to be all this mumbo-jumbo——

ALEXANDER. The mumbo-jumbo, as you call it, is very important. The Great King of Persia is taking a wife and the ceremony must be carried out according to the rites and usages of his Persian ancestors——

CLEITUS. His Persian ancestors? Holy Gods above! That I should live to hear such words spoken by the son of Philip—

ALEXANDER [*quietly*]. Get him out of here.

PTOLEMY. Cleitus—come away——

CLEITUS [*shaking off* PTOLEMY]. His Persian ancestors! It's a pity your Persian ancestors lost the battle of Marathon, isn't it? Then they might have saved us all this fighting we've been doing these last eight years.

HEPHAESTION. Stop it, Cleitus, for the love of God! The King didn't mean——

CLEITUS. I know what the King meant. He meant that he's forgotten he's the Captain-General of Greece.

ALEXANDER [*to* HEPHAESTION]. This is the man who talks about barbarians. I tell you that girl there is a hundred times more civilised than he is——

HEPHAESTION. Let me take his part in the ceremony, and he can take mine——

ALEXANDER. Yes, all right. But get him out of here now. His boorishness offends me——

CLEITUS. Yes, Great King and Master of the World, I'll go. And I'll carry your crown for you this evening. But, by God, I won't kneel in the mud in front of you either. I'm a freeborn Macedonian and I'd sooner die——

ALEXANDER [*now furious*]. That alternative may not be so difficult to arrange——

CLEITUS. Oh yes. I don't doubt you can have me murdered as you had Parmenion—— [ALEXANDER *throws the contents of his cup in* CLEITUS' *face.* HEPHAESTION *and* PTOLEMY *pinion* CLEITUS' *arms.*] If you don't like the truth don't ask Macedonians to drink with you. Stick to your Persian slaves——

ALEXANDER [*through his teeth*]. Take him out or I'll kill him.

CLEITUS *is forced towards the tent entrance by* HEPHAESTION *and* PTOLEMY. *He breaks free for a moment and faces* ALEXANDER.

CLEITUS. Thank God Philip isn't alive today to see the shame of his son——

With a sob ALEXANDER *draws his sword and runs at* CLEITUS. HEPHAESTION *leaps at his arm and knocks the sword out of his hand.*

ALEXANDER. Let me go!

PTOLEMY *forces* CLEITUS *out of the tent.*

CLEITUS [*shouting as he goes*]. Unlike his son—Philip, at least, was a man——

ALEXANDER [*shouting*]. Guard! Guard! [A SENTRY *runs in.*] Call out the guard, I say! Kill Cleitus——

ALEXANDER *has flung himself free of* HEPHAESTION *and as the* SENTRY *hesitates he snatches his javelin from him and runs to the tent entrance. There he poises himself for a careful aim and hurls the javelin. Having thrown it he remains motionless a moment—then retreats two steps into the tent.* CLEITUS *suddenly appears in the tent entrance, staring at* ALEXANDER, *surprised, with wide eyes.*

CLEITUS. Alexander—it's only that I'm rather drunk—you shouldn't have thought—I really meant——

He staggers and topples over, face downwards, on to the floor. A javelin is deeply transfixed into his back. PTOLEMY, *startled and afraid, has appeared in the tent entrance.* ROXANA *is cowering into a corner.* ALEXANDER *kneels down by* CLEITUS, HEPHAESTION *at his side.*

ALEXANDER [*whispering*]. This has happened before. The wedding banquet. I've killed my father. He tried to kill me, didn't he? He came at me with his sword and slipped. You saw it, didn't you, Hephaestion? [*With a sudden loud cry.*] I've killed my father. Parricide! I'm a parricide and I must die—— [*He jumps up and runs to the table, snatching up a knife and turning it against his throat.*] I've killed my father and I must die.

HEPHAESTION *gives him two savage blows with either fist on the chin.* ALEXANDER *collapses on to a divan.*

HEPHAESTION [*to* PTOLEMY]. Help me carry him.

THE LIGHTS FADE

SCENE FIVE

ALEXANDER'S *tent. It is night and the tent is lit by lamplight. It has been stripped of ornaments and fittings.* TWO SOLDIERS *are engaged in carrying out a chest, supervised by* HEPHAESTION.

HEPHAESTION. Careful with that, now. It has breakables.

SOLDIER. Yes, sir.

HEPHAESTION. It's to go on the King's personal baggage cart.

SOLDIER. Yes, sir. What about this? [*He kicks another chest.*]

HEPHAESTION. That can go with the other heavy stuff.

SOLDIER. Very good.

They carry the chest out, as PERDICCAS *comes in.*

HEPHAESTION. Perdiccas—thank God you're back. I thought you were going to miss us.

PERDICCAS. What's going on? Why are you breaking camp?

HEPHAESTION. India.

PERDICCAS. India? But that wasn't to be for another six weeks.

HEPHAESTION. It's tomorrow at first light.

PERDICCAS. But that's madness. It's far too early in the year to cross those mountains. Even the foothills will still be snowed up.

HEPHAESTION. We must hope the Gods are kind.

PERDICCAS. What's happened? What's made him change his mind like this?

HEPHAESTION. I don't know.

PERDICCAS. Cleitus?

HEPHAESTION. You heard about that did you?

PERDICCAS. Yes. We caught a couple of deserters. Most unfortunate, that business. It'll have had a bad effect on the army. [*The* SOLDIERS *have re-entered and are now carrying out the other chest.*] Was Alexander going to move off without waiting for us, then?

HEPHAESTION. Yes. You're three days late.

PERDICCAS. Not our fault. You should see what the rivers are like. What's going to happen to the Queen-Mother, then? Are we to leave her in this place—Alexander-at-the-end-of-the-World, or whatever it's called?

HEPHAESTION [*shortly*]. She's to follow the march to India.

PERDICCAS. God above! She'll never survive that.

HEPHAESTION. I know. I've told him so—many times.

PERDICCAS. What's the matter with him? Gone off his head or something?

HEPHAESTION. How was your commission?

PERDICCAS. Pretty horrible. Necessary, of course. I realized that. Still, I can't say I enjoyed it.

HEPHAESTION. It was successful anyway?

PERDICCAS. Oh yes, It looked ugly for a moment or so. But Alexander's proclamation did the trick.

ALEXANDER *comes in.*

ALEXANDER [*seeing* PERDICCAS]. Perdiccas? [*Harshly.*] You've saved yourself a court-martial by a matter of hours.

PERDICCAS. I'm sorry, sir. The rivers are in flood and I didn't care to take risks because of the Queen-Mother.

ALEXANDER. Where is she?

PERDICCAS. I arranged her old accommodation——

ALEXANDER. Bring her here——

PERDICCAS. She might be asleep, sir——

ALEXANDER. So might I, but I'm not. Bring her here.

PERDICCAS. Yes, sir.

He goes out.

ALEXANDER. How long to dawn, Hephaestion?

HEPHAESTION. About two hours.

ALEXANDER. God, but this night seems endless. I've lost my copy of Homer. Have you seen it?

HEPHAESTION. No, sir.

ALEXANDER. I might have lent it to Cleitus. I think I did. Have his things searched for it.

HEPHAESTION. I'll lend you mine.

ALEXANDER. I want mine. It has my notes. Besides, it's a mascot.

HEPHAESTION. I see. I'll find it for you.

ALEXANDER. You know the order of march?

HEPHAESTION. Yes, sir. I've been over it many times.

ALEXANDER. See that the men take the usual precautions against frostbite.

HEPHAESTION. Yes. Those orders were issued.

ALEXANDER. I shall ride Bucephalus tomorrow—as if we were going into battle.

HEPHAESTION. Yes, sir.

ALEXANDER. Yes. I shall ride Bucephalus again . . . Poor old Bucephalus. [*The* QUEEN-MOTHER *comes in. Her expression is calm and impassive and her eyes are on the ground. She looks much as she did when she was brought into* ALEXANDER'S *tent after Issus.* PERDICCAS *enters behind her.*] [*To* HEPHAESTION *and* PERDICCAS.] All right. Leave me. [*To* HEPHAESTION.] See that we're not disturbed.

HEPHAESTION. Yes, sir. [*To* QUEEN-MOTHER.] May I say, ma'am, how very glad I am that you are here—even in these circumstances?

The QUEEN-MOTHER *bows slightly, without taking her eyes from the ground.* HEPHAESTION *goes out. She kneels down and lays her forehead to the ground.* ALEXANDER *stops short, frowning.*

ALEXANDER. We're not at court. You're in my tent alone, and there's no one watching us. [*Angrily.*] Get up. You look ridiculous. [*She rises.*] I apologise for the discomforts of your journey. I hope they weren't too great? [*The* QUEEN-MOTHER *shakes her head quietly.*] I see. You're going to keep your vow, then? Very well, as you please. I've no doubt that there will be moments on the march through the Himalayas to India when you may feel inclined to break your decorous silence. [*She shows no emotion at this.*] Yes, madam, India. You don't suppose I'd be fool enough to leave an avowed enemy behind me in Babylon—an enemy who can still command some allegiance from her former subjects? I may be as mad as people say I am, but I'm not as mad as that. [*He pours himself a cup of wine.*] Some wine? [*She shakes her head.*] Perhaps you'll forgive me if I do. Since I saw you last I have rather taken to the drinking of wine. I've no doubt in Babylon you've been hearing rumours that I've become a drunkard—but that isn't true. Wine doesn't make me drunk—it makes me more clearheaded. What is that you are holding in your hand? [*She opens her hand and discloses a locket with a chain.*] What is it? A locket? For me? [*She nods her head. He takes the locket from her hand.*] Thank you. I seem to recognise this. Yes, I do. [*He examines it.*] I remember now—it belonged to my father—he gave it to someone—[*He suddenly throws the locket away violently, and seems for a moment to find some difficulty in speaking.*] It's dangerous, you know, to do such things to me in my present mood. I killed a man the other day—with my own hands—for less. You'd better go. [*She kneels to pick up the locket.*] No. Don't pick it up. Let it lie there and rot—like its master's body. Go. Be ready to leave in two hours. [*She rises. Just as she reaches the tent opening* ALEXANDER *speaks in a gentle, pleading voice.*] Mother. Mother, turn round. [*She turns.*] Look at me, mother. Please look at me. [*She shakes her head.*] You are my prisoner and I command you. Lift your eyes and look at me. [*She looks up slowly and gazes at him.*] What do you see? Tell me. Am I so very changed? Is this still the Alexander you used to know? Tell me—what am I to do? Only you can tell me that. No one else. Speak to me, mother. Speak to me.

QUEEN-MOTHER. Alexander——

ALEXANDER *begins to sob on her shoulder, like a small boy. She smooths his head.*

ALEXANDER. Oh thank you, mother. Thank you.

QUEEN-MOTHER. You're not so very changed, Alexander.

She sits on a stool.

ALEXANDER. I *am* changed. I know it, but there's nothing I could have done to save myself. I swear that, mother.

QUEEN-MOTHER. No, I always knew that. Once you had started you had to go on. There was no turning back.

ALEXANDER. Before Gaugemela I could have turned back.

QUEEN-MOTHER. Yes. Before Gaugemela you could.

ALEXANDER. You suggested it—do you remember—that you should walk a mile through the darkness to the Persian camp—to make peace with your son? Why didn't I let you do that? Everything would have been all right then—I know.

QUEEN-MOTHER. I don't think it would. The devil that's in you wouldn't have let you rest.

ALEXANDER. Can I kill the devil that's in me? Could I ever have killed him?

QUEEN-MOTHER. Perhaps, once—a long time ago. Perhaps if I'd been your real mother I could have killed him for you.

ALEXANDER. "Know yourself"—that's what the Pythia said. The first conquest is yourself, she said. Only after that—the world.

QUEEN-MOTHER. The Pythia was a wise woman.

ALEXANDER. What am I to do now?

QUEEN-MOTHER. Go on to the bitter end.

ALEXANDER. Will the end be bitter?

QUEEN-MOTHER. Yes.

ALEXANDER. Why must it be?

QUEEN-MOTHER. Because you are Alexander. Your devil will conquer you.

ALEXANDER. What does it matter if I do lose my soul—provided I conquer the world? I'm Alexander the Conqueror. I shall be remembered not for what I am but for what I do.

QUEEN-MOTHER. But what you do makes you what you are.

ALEXANDER. Let it. I'm ready for the sacrifice. It's only being alone that makes me miserable and afraid. Now you're with me I feel brave again. And tomorrow, India. I shall conquer India, mother.

QUEEN-MOTHER. Yes, my son. I've no doubt you will.

ALEXANDER. And after India—the west—and after the west—the north. There's plenty yet to do. I must have action. When the Gods give me action I'm happy. No time for thinking—doing—doing—doing. That's all that matters in this world.

QUEEN-MOTHER. That's all that matters in Alexander's world.

ALEXANDER. Alexander's world is good enough for Alexander. For him it's the best world there is.

QUEEN-MOTHER. Perhaps because he knows no other.

ALEXANDER. Well, if he did know another, he'd conquer it. Mother, give me your blessing.

He kneels before her and she kisses him on the forehead.

QUEEN-MOTHER. Bless you, my son.

PERDICCAS *comes in.*

PERDICCAS. I humbly beg pardon, sir—but I've been told to

present a petition to you from the second division of Thessalonian Horse. As they were the first contingent across the Hellespont they beg to be allowed the honour of leading the march on India.

ALEXANDER. Their request is granted.

PERDICCAS. Yes, sir——

ALEXANDER. And Perdiccas. You will join us in India at the earliest opportunity.

PERDICCAS. Join you?

ALEXANDER. Yes. From Babylon.

PERDICCAS. But I've just come from Babylon.

ALEXANDER. And you're going back there tomorrow. You're to escort the Queen-Mother.

PERDICCAS. God above! It's all of a thousand miles——

ALEXANDER. All right, Perdiccas.

PERDICCAS. Yes, sir.

He goes out.

ALEXANDER. Will you go back to your quarters now?

QUEEN-MOTHER. Yes, Alexander.

ALEXANDER *opens the tent flap for her.*

ALEXANDER. I shall come to your tent to say goodbye. And to thank you.

QUEEN-MOTHER. For what?

ALEXANDER. For breaking your vow.

QUEEN-MOTHER. My vow? I'd forgotten my vow. [*With a sigh.*] Another conquest for Alexander.

ALEXANDER. The greatest he will ever make—by far.

He kisses her hand and she goes out.

HEPHAESTION *comes in.*

ALEXANDER. Hephaestion—I have some new orders for you.

HEPHAESTION. Yes, sir.

ALEXANDER. And don't call me sir. You know it annoys me—from you. I've noticed the men have accumulated far too much baggage——

HEPHAESTION. Yes—I've spoken to the under-officers about it but——

ALEXANDER. But they say that if Alexander has twenty cartloads why shouldn't they have one?

HEPHAESTION. I've reasoned with them.

ALEXANDER. Well, don't reason with them any more. I tell you what we'll do. You and I will go out now and make an enormous bonfire—like the bonfires we used to make as boys—do you remember?

HEPHAESTION. As well as you do.

ALEXANDER. We'll throw all those twenty cartloads on to it, one by one—and last of all we'll throw this tent——

HEPHAESTION. This tent?

ALEXANDER. Yes. It should make a beautiful bonfire, don't you agree? And on top of it all I shall put that throne.

HEPHAESTION. Yes. I should like to see that throne on a bonfire.

ALEXANDER. But will it burn, do you think?

HEPHAESTION. I pray to God it will.

ALEXANDER. And so do I, Hephaestion. So do I.

THE LIGHTS FADE

EPILOGUE

Before the lights come up ALEXANDER'S *voice can be heard—as in the prologue, though a whisper, filling the theatre with sound.*

ALEXANDER'S VOICE. But it didn't burn. There is no way of burning a conquered throne. Hephaestion? Hephaestion? Where are you? Hephaestion? But, of course, you are dead, aren't you? When did you die? Was it in India? No, it was after India. You were at my side as we sailed down the Indus—crowned with the laurels of victory—do you remember, Hephaestion? What did you die of? A fever they said, didn't they? Was it a fever, or was it a broken heart? [*The lights come on, revealing the same scene as in the prologue, with the same people surrounding the bed. A* SOLDIER *is just saluting and the hand is weakly raised in reply. The* SOLDIER *goes out. Another takes his place.*] I remember you, my friend. A good Phalanxman. I decorated you once. What are you weeping for? Now you can go home to Macedon. Or have you a wife here, in Babylon? Anyway, goodbye. [*The* SOLDIER *goes out. A third takes his place.*] Can this really be the end? God—oh God—this is a brutal joke you are playing. The conqueror of the world dies of a chill at the age of thirty-two. How my father, Philip, must be chuckling to himself now. It doesn't matter. I've shown him, haven't I? I've shown him.

The SOLDIER *goes out.*

PTOLEMY. That's the last.

PERDICCAS. I'll tell Craterus.

PTOLEMY. Yes. I'd better have another try to get an answer out of him. [PERDICCAS *goes out.* PTOLEMY *approaches the bed.*] Sir? Sir? Do you hear me? Make a sign if you understand. [*The hand is raised again.*] Alexander—will you say who is to succeed you on the throne of Asia? Who is to be Master of the World?

ALEXANDER'S VOICE. Who is to be the Master of the World? Who shall I condemn to death?

PTOLEMY. His lips moved again—but I heard nothing. Repeat that, sir——

ALEXANDER'S VOICE. Who shall I condemn to death? No one. This will be my last act of mercy. Let them fight it out for themselves. Goodbye then. The adventure is over and the adventurer would like to go to sleep.

CURTAIN